Level 3

Academic Vocabulary

25 Content-Area Lessons

Author
Christine Dugan, M.A.Ed.

Publishing Credits

Dona Herweck Rice, *Editor-in-Chief*; Lee Aucoin, *Creative Director*; Don Tran, *Print Production Manager*; Timothy J. Bradley, *Illustration Manager*; Conni Medina, M.A.Ed., *Editorial Director*; Sara Johnson, M.S.Ed., *Senior Editor*, Evelyn Garcia, *Associate Education Editor*; Juan Chavolla, *Designer*; Corinne Burton, M.A.Ed., *Publisher*

Shell Education
5301 Oceanus Drive
Huntington Beach, CA 92649-1030
http://www.shelleducation.com

ISBN 978-1-4258-0705-4

Table of Contents

Research

This series, *Academic Vocabulary: 25 Content-Area Lessons*, provides ready-to-use lessons that help teachers develop effective strategies that build vocabulary and conceptual understanding in all content areas. Vocabulary knowledge is a key component of reading comprehension and is strongly related to general academic achievement (Feldman and Kinsella 2005). Students need to understand key academic vocabulary that crosses all content areas to fully develop conceptual understanding.

What Is Vocabulary Knowledge?

Simply put, *vocabulary knowledge* means having an awareness of words and word meanings. Yet, vocabulary skills are more complicated than simply reciting key terms and their definitions.

Vocabulary knowledge is often described as *receptive* or *expressive*. *Receptive vocabulary* includes words that we recognize when heard or seen. *Expressive vocabulary* includes words that we use when we speak or write. Students typically have a larger receptive vocabulary than expressive vocabulary (Lehr, Osborn, and Hiebert 2004); they are familiar with many words, but may not understand their multiple definitions or the deeper nuances of how those words are used in oral and written language.

So, then, what does it mean for a student to truly know a word? Beck, McKeown, and Kucan (2002) state that word knowledge is not black and white; understanding vocabulary is not as simple as either knowing a word or not. The process by which students learn new words is complex and often occurs in progression. Word knowledge may range from students never having heard of a word, to students understanding all there is to know about a word, or some level of understanding that lies between the two extremes. Understanding this complexity of word knowledge helps educators develop a vocabulary program that addresses these unique learning processes. The lessons in this book support both receptive and expressive vocabulary.

What Is Academic Vocabulary?

Specialized content vocabulary, although distinct, is considered a part of academic vocabulary. Yopp, Yopp, and Bishop (2009) have developed definitions for each category. ***Specialized content vocabulary*** words are specific to a particular content area and represent important concepts or ideas. Examples of these include *boycott* (social studies), *habitat* (science), *numerator* (mathematics), *autobiography* (reading), and *narrative* (writing). ***General academic vocabulary*** includes high-utility words found across content areas and throughout students' academic reading, writing, and speech experiences. Words such as *explain*, *define*, *identify*, and *organize* are examples of general academic vocabulary.

Research *(cont.)*

Why Teach Academic Vocabulary?

Yopp, Yopp, and Bishop (2009) have synthesized the importance of teaching academic vocabulary, and there is evidence that instruction in vocabulary positively affects reading comprehension. In order to read a written language successfully, we need to understand the words the author has chosen. Research confirms that vocabulary knowledge is positively related to a student's ability to comprehend text (Lehr, Osborn, and Hiebert 2004); thus, the relationship between word knowledge and comprehension is clear.

Vocabulary knowledge is crucial for success in reading; however, its influence does not stop there. It also plays a significant role in overall academic success (Lehr, Osborn, and Hiebert 2004). Students' knowledge of words impacts their achievement in all areas of the curriculum because words are necessary in communicating the content. Understanding and expressing the concepts and principles of content areas requires knowledge of the specialized vocabulary that represents those specific concepts and principles.

Indeed, Marzano (2004) maintains that there is a strong relationship between vocabulary knowledge and background knowledge. As a result, building students' vocabulary increases their background knowledge, thereby providing more opportunities for learning new concepts. The lessons in this book offer purposeful opportunities to build students' vocabulary while learning the new concepts within the content areas.

Best Practices

Teaching vocabulary is critical for helping students increase their oral vocabulary, enhance their reading comprehension, and extend their writing skills. Yet, in order for students to benefit from their word knowledge, it is not enough for teachers to simply introduce new vocabulary and share definitions. In short, the quality of a vocabulary program matters.

Research shows that there are several components of an effective vocabulary program:

- regular opportunities to develop oral language (Nagy 2005)
- a culture of promoting word consciousness (Nagy and Scott 2000)
- dynamic, explicit instruction of key words (Beck, McKeown, and Kucan 2002)
- guidance in independent word-learning strategies (Graves 2000)
- daily structured contexts for academic word use in speaking, writing, and assessment (Beck, McKeown, and Kucan 2002)
- students' fluent reading of varied text (Cunningham and Stanovich 1998)

How To Use This Book

Academic Vocabulary: 25 Content-Area Lessons provides teachers with lessons that integrate academic vocabulary instruction into content-area lessons. This book includes 25 step-by-step, standards-based lessons. Each lesson features two vocabulary-development strategies that reflect the latest research in effective vocabulary instruction. The strategies within each lesson vary and are presented in detail on pages 8–31 and address the following key aspects of effective vocabulary instruction:

Developing Oral Language	Developing Word Consciousness
Developing students' oral language skills is crucial to assist them in navigating school texts and understanding more complex oral and written patterns of language. These strategies help students gain a deeper understanding of academic words and concepts by guiding them to use the words in a meaningful way.	These strategies provide structured opportunities to build students' awareness of academic words used in the classroom and their lives. Students are encouraged to note when they see or hear key words and to use the words themselves. This strategy helps students develop a true love of language and a keen sense of how words sound as they hear and speak them.
Teaching Words	**Independent Word Learning**
These strategies use a variety of techniques to help students build conceptual knowledge and increase their oral and written vocabularies. This type of strategy may be incorporated at different points throughout your study. Some of the strategies are more effective in introducing new words while others will benefit students as they review and make connections among words.	These strategies help students derive word meanings and explore the use of context to infer the meaning of unknown words. The strategies can be taught and reviewed throughout the school year to improve students' abilities in learning words independently.

How To Use This Book *(cont.)*

Each two-page lesson is followed by two student activity pages as well as an assessment that allows teachers to assess students' vocabulary knowledge in effective and meaningful ways. All of the reproducible student activity pages are also included on the Teacher Resource CD.

Each lesson in this book includes two **featured academic vocabulary strategies**. An overview of each strategy can be found on pages 8–31.

Specialized content vocabulary and **general academic vocabulary** words are identified at the beginning of the lesson.

The **standards** listed in each lesson indicate the area of focus for the lesson.

Each lesson includes a **differentiation** section to help meet the needs of all students.

The **materials** needed to complete the lesson are listed.

The **procedures** provide step-by-step instructions for teaching the content-area lesson.

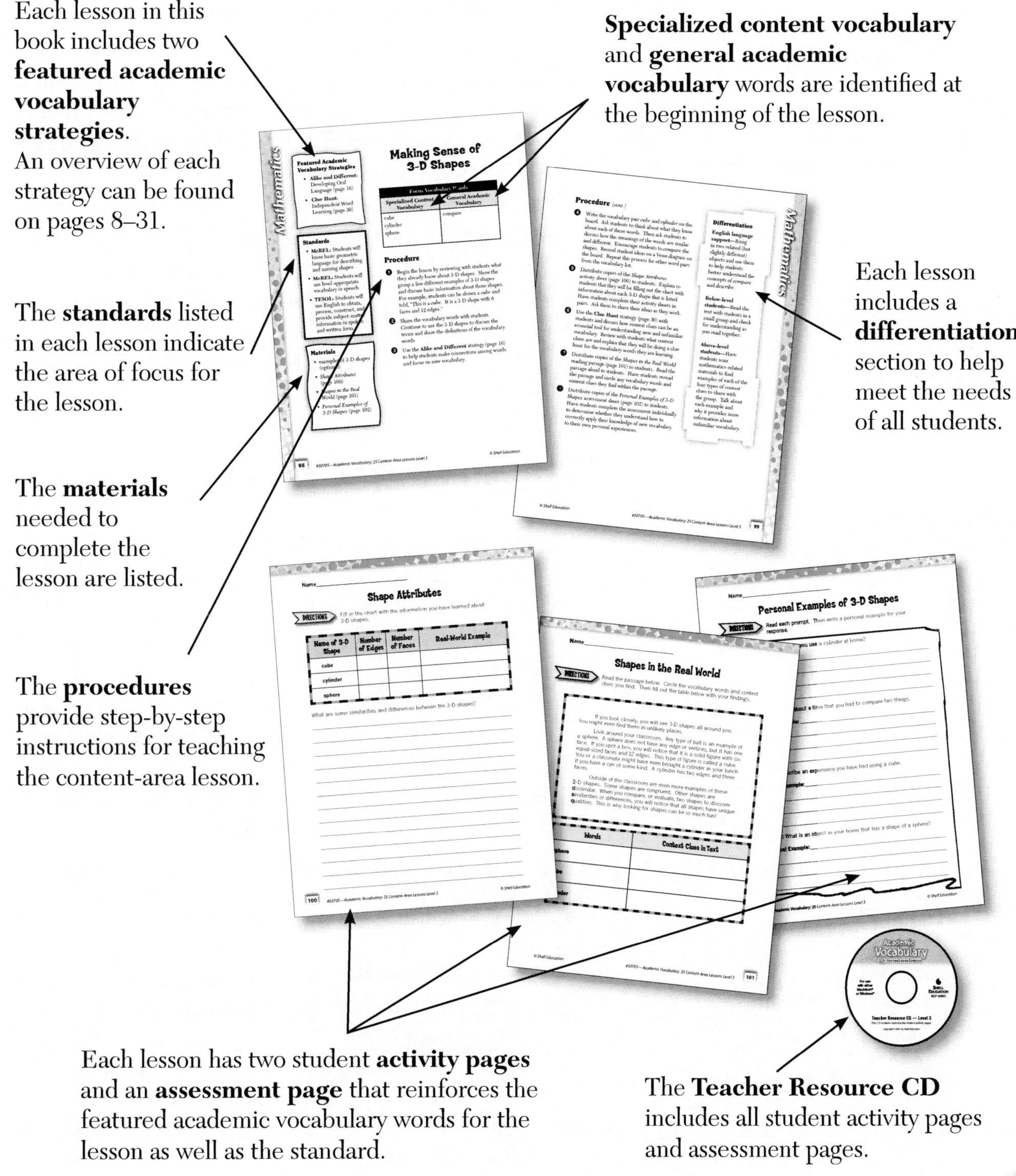

Each lesson has two student **activity pages** and an **assessment page** that reinforces the featured academic vocabulary words for the lesson as well as the standard.

The **Teacher Resource CD** includes all student activity pages and assessment pages.

Strategy Category:

Developing Oral Language

Materials

- paper bag filled with items related to an upcoming unit of study

Mystery Bag

What Is It?

The Mystery Bag strategy (Yopp, Yopp, and Bishop 2009) helps students develop oral language skills by sparking conversations about a topic. The teacher fills a paper bag with objects that relate to an upcoming lesson and reflect the focus vocabulary words. As the teacher pulls each object from the bag, students identify and discuss it. They are encouraged to draw upon their knowledge about the object. For example, if a newspaper is drawn from the bag, students would name the object and discuss its use. This process is repeated with the second object in the bag. The students then brainstorm how the two objects are related and why both items are in the same bag. This process continues with all of the objects in the bag.

When and Why Do I Use It?

The Mystery Bag strategy should be used at the beginning of a lesson to activate prior knowledge and to build background knowledge. Real objects, not just pictures, are used so that students can see and touch them. This hands-on, kinesthetic activity is excellent for English language learners because it provides them with objects to connect the vocabulary that they are learning. The mystery about the object in the bag, the opportunity to see and touch the items, and the time given to discuss them generates great interest in a new topic.

Example

For a social studies lesson on regions, items that can be included in a mystery bag could include the following:

- small cactus plant
- articles of clothing that can be worn in the different regions (e.g., sunglasses for desert, scarf for mountains)

How Does It Work?

1. To prepare for this strategy, decide on the topic of focus for the mystery bag. Gather objects related to the topic and place these items in a bag. Make a list of vocabulary words that you want students to know, based on the topic. These can be specialized content and/or general academic words.
2. To begin the lesson, gather students so they can all easily see the mystery bag. Do not tell students the new topic of study. This is what keeps the "mystery" exciting!
3. Pull one object from the bag. Ask students to identify the object. Then encourage students to describe the object and explain what they know about it. Students should draw upon their experiences with the object. Pass the object around so that all students can see and touch it.
4. Remove a second object from the bag and pass it around the class. Ask students to identify the object. Then encourage students to describe the object. This time, ask students to try to explain how the two objects are related.
5. Continue this discussion until all of the objects have been pulled from the bag, passed around, named, and discussed. Write the following question words on the board: *What? When? Where? Why? Who? How?* Encourage students to use these words to ask questions about the objects. Record the list of questions on the board.
6. Ask students to try to name the new topic of study, based on the collection of objects. Once the topic has been identified, write it on the board. Then review each object in the bag and name the academic vocabulary word(s) associated with it.
7. Finally, ask students to brainstorm other vocabulary words associated with this topic, using the objects from the bag for ideas. Write the words that students suggest on the board and use the list as a reference throughout the lesson or unit.

Differentiation

English language support—Work with a small group of students to provide additional background information about the lesson. Read a book with strong picture connections to explain the topic. If possible, show short video clips from the Internet.

Below-level students—Pass around the objects from the bag. As each student holds an object, say the name of the object. Ask students to repeat the names of the objects. Then use the name of each object in a sentence and ask students to repeat after you.

Above-level students—Ask students to sort and classify the objects into subgroups and then explain their reasoning for sorting this way. Ask students what other objects could be added to the bag and to describe why these additional items make good connections.

Strategy Category:

Developing Oral Language

Materials

- none

Have You Ever?

What Is It?

Have You Ever? (Beck, McKeown, and Kucan 2002) is a strategy that helps students connect their knowledge of important vocabulary words to their own personal experiences. Take the example of the word *compare*. Rather than simply asking students to recite a dictionary definition of the word, students can make more personal connections to the word if they answer a relevant question, such as, "Describe a time when you might *compare* two things."

When and Why Do I Use It?

The Have You Ever? strategy can be used just after students have been introduced to a new word or group of words and have a basic understanding of the word(s). It is effective for both specialized content and general academic words. This strategy is intended to help further students' understanding of new words and broaden the contexts in which they might use them. This approach to learning new words requires that students use vocabulary in context to answer questions and discuss suggested topics. It helps students see that these words can be a real and meaningful part of their vernacular.

Example

For a language arts lesson on descriptive writing, questions that can be asked include the following:

- What special event can you write about in *sequential order*?
- What topic from your own life can you *describe* in a paragraph?

How Does It Work?

1. Before using this strategy, decide which vocabulary words to use. You can use specialized content and/or general academic words. The words must already have been introduced to students.

2. To prepare for using the strategy, decide how these words may be related to the students' personal experiences and backgrounds. Consider how you might frame questions that get students to use these words in the context of their lives.

3. Write the selected vocabulary words on the board. Remind students that they have already learned something about these words. Explain to students that they will use the words to talk about their experiences. Model the process by choosing one word and telling a personal anecdote related to it.

4. Divide students into groups of three. Ask one question for each word that includes the term. These questions should help students use the words correctly as they describe their personal experiences. Questions may begin as follows:
   - *Have you ever…?*
   - *Describe a time when…*
   - *What did it feel like to…?*
   - *What do you remember about…?*

5. After posing each question, give each student time to share thoughts and ideas in their small groups. Guide students in using the vocabulary word in their responses. Write sentence frames on the board to help students formulate their responses. Then have a few students share their ideas with the class.

6. Once students are familiar with this strategy and can orally share their knowledge of the vocabulary, change this strategy to a written activity. Provide students with sentence frames and have them write their ideas.

7. In conclusion, ask students how thinking about the connections these words have to their lives helps them better understand the words' meanings.

Differentiation

English language support—Consider student backgrounds and histories as you write questions and sentence frames for this strategy. Also, provide appropriate sentence frames for students to complete.

Below-level students—Provide additional modeling and share anecdotes related to each word in multiple contexts. These extra examples can help students relate the vocabulary words to their experiences.

Above-level students—Extend this activity to have students consider not only their own perspectives related to a vocabulary word but also the perspectives of others.

Strategy Category:

Developing Oral Language

Materials

- none

Questions, Reasons, and Examples

What Is It?

When using Questions, Reasons, and Examples (Beck, McKeown, and Kucan 2002), teachers discuss each vocabulary word in the form of questions, reasons, and examples. Students then reply with comments, questions, examples, answers, and other kinds of responses.

When and Why Do I Use It?

Questions, Reasons, and Examples should be used to help develop students' understanding of the words after they have been introduced to the selected vocabulary words. This strategy helps students interact with new vocabulary words by hearing relevant examples of the words in use. However, students must also share information related to the words and generate their own examples. This strategy works with both specialized content and general academic words.

Example

For a mathematics lesson on fractions, *fraction* can be described as a part of a whole. The teacher can then ask the following questions:

- When was a time that you had to divide something into a *fraction* to share with a friend?
- What are some examples of food you have seen cut into *fractions*?

Then an example can be given to students such as, "An example of a *fraction* is a pizza. It is divided into equal parts. When I take a slice, I am taking part of a whole."

How Does It Work?

1. Before using this strategy, identify the vocabulary words that will be the focus of this lesson. Specialized content and/or general academic words can be selected.
2. Decide how these words can be used in meaningful contexts. What kinds of examples might students relate to and understand? What questions can use the vocabulary words in meaningful ways? What examples can students provide for the words? Use these ideas to formulate questions about the words that require students to answer in an appropriate context, justify their answers, and identify examples.
3. Review the vocabulary words with students. Say each word aloud and then have students repeat your pronunciation. Share a student-friendly definition of each word. Give clear and relevant examples of each.
4. After presenting each word, write the questions for it on the board. Under each question, write a sentence frame that will help students answer the question in a complete sentence that includes the selected vocabulary word. Read each question aloud. Model how to use the sentence frame to answer the questions.
5. Divide students into pairs. Give students time to discuss the words and questions and to respond orally with their partners.
6. Have a few student volunteers elaborate on their ideas and responses to the questions. Write responses on the board to complete the sentence frames. Discuss these ideas as a group.
7. To conclude the strategy, ask students how the strategy is helpful for reviewing and remembering vocabulary.

Differentiation

English language support—Let students draw examples of each word when appropriate. Then use students' drawings to help them formulate their responses in complete sentences.

Below-level students—When asking students for examples of a word, provide two choices (one correct and one incorrect). Narrow the scope of this part of the strategy for students until they have developed a deeper understanding of each word. When students are ready, encourage them to identify their own examples.

Above-level students—Extend this activity by having students sort into meaningful groups the reasons and examples shared by the class.

Strategy Category:

Developing Oral Language

Materials

- none

Cloze Sentences

What Is It?

For the Cloze Sentences strategy (Beck, McKeown, and Kucan 2002), students must choose academic vocabulary words to fit into cloze sentences. The teacher reads aloud the cloze sentences before asking students to complete them with appropriate vocabulary words. Students can complete the cloze sentences individually, in pairs, in small groups, or as a whole class.

When and Why Do I Use It?

Cloze sentences can be used to reinforce an introduction of vocabulary words. This strategy is effective for both specialized content and general academic words.

Example

For a science lesson on the planets, some examples of cloze sentences include the following:

- We can use a ________ to help magnify distant objects such as stars in the sky. *(telescope)*
- The planet we live on is ________, and it is third from the sun. *(Earth)*

How Does It Work?

1. Identify the specialized content and/or general academic vocabulary words that will be the focus of the lesson. These should be words to which the students have been introduced but that still need additional reinforcement.
2. Write cloze sentences that help students see how to use the vocabulary words appropriately. Make sure the sentences provide enough context for students to identify the selected vocabulary words that correctly complete the sentences. Record these sentences on a sheet of chart paper or on the board.
3. Write the selected vocabulary words on the board. Read each word aloud and ask students to repeat after you. Say each word again and ask students to clap once for each syllable. Then briefly review the meaning of each word.
4. Read the cloze sentences aloud. Ask students to share which word they think will best complete the sentence. Discuss the clues in the sentence that support students' understanding of the words. Have students read the completed sentences.
5. Repeat this process with the remaining cloze sentences.
6. To conclude the strategy, review the cloze sentences and talk about how students completed them.

Differentiation

English language support—Whenever possible, create appropriately leveled cloze sentences. For example, you may wish to provide several short cloze sentences for one vocabulary word.

Below-level students—Provide students with a small word bank of two or three words at the end of each sentence. Have students use the word banks to complete the cloze sentences.

Above-level students—Ask students to write another set of cloze sentences using the selected vocabulary words. They can trade their sentences and work in pairs to read them aloud and fill them in with the appropriate words.

Strategy Category:

Developing Oral Language

Materials

- none

Alike and Different

What Is It?

The Alike and Different strategy (Beck, McKeown, and Kucan 2002) gives students an opportunity to determine how vocabulary words are both alike and different. This activity can be either oral or written and can be completed individually, in pairs, in small groups, or as a whole class. No matter how the strategy is organized, allow time for students to talk about the words, the connections among words, and why students identified those connections.

When and Why Do I Use It?

This strategy should be used after students have been introduced to a group of vocabulary words. This strategy requires students to analyze the critical aspects of key words and concepts, and therefore deepens their understanding of new words. The strategy can be used with both specialized content and general academic words.

Example

For a mathematics lesson on multiplication, the word pairs *multiplication* and *addition* can be used to demonstrate how the words are alike and different. A Venn diagram can be incorporated into this strategy so students can see the comparison between both words. The following is an example of a completed Venn diagram:

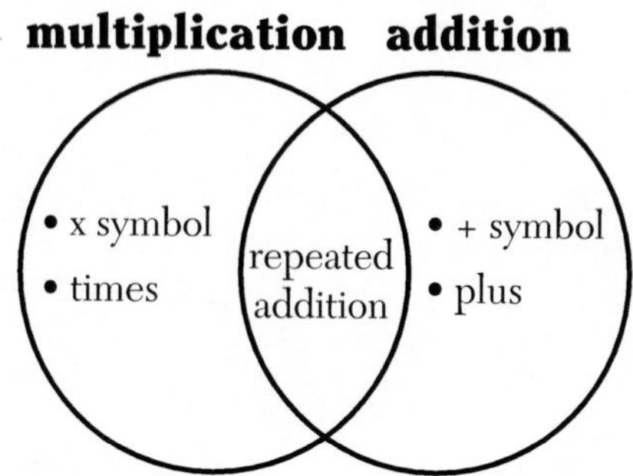

How Does It Work?

1. Identify the specialized content and/or general academic vocabulary words that will be the focus of the lesson. These should be words that students are familiar with but that they are still learning.
2. Pair words in a way that makes sense. Ask students to consider how the two words are both alike and different. Write the word pairs on the board.
3. Read the first pair of words aloud and then ask students to repeat after you. Ask students to tell what they already know about each word in the first pair. List their responses on the board next to the word pair. Or, you may organize the information in a Venn diagram.
4. Ask students to think about and discuss how the words are alike. Students can make connections individually, in pairs, in small groups, or as a whole class. Organize this strategy in the way that best meets the needs of your students.
5. Ask students to think about how the words are different.
6. Continue reading the pairs of words and discussing their similarities and differences. To conclude the strategy, review the pairs and talk about how the words are both alike and different.

Differentiation

English language support—Have students draw what they know about each word. Encourage them to label their drawings with the appropriate vocabulary word(s).

Below-level students—Lead students to thoroughly brainstorm what they already know about each word. Chart their responses in a way that will make sense to students (e.g., a Venn diagram, a T-chart). Then guide students in using the charted information to tell how the words are alike and different.

Above-level students—Give students a list of focus words and challenge them to make pairs themselves. Then ask them to share orally why they paired certain words and how the words are both alike and different.

Strategy Category:

Developing Oral Language

Materials

- none

Idea Completions

What Is It?

Idea Completions are sentence starters that require students to incorporate a word's definition into a meaningful context (Beck, McKeown, and Kucan 2002).

When and Why Do I Use It?

Idea Completions can be used just after introducing new vocabulary words to students. This strategy can be used with both specialized content and general academic words. Students must practice using vocabulary words in appropriate ways. When students are asked to write sentences that only include vocabulary words, the resulting sentences often contain vague or insignificant uses of the new vocabulary word. These Idea Completion sentences must be written in such a way that students are guided to use vocabulary words appropriately and in context within sentences that are semantically accurate.

Example

For a language arts lesson on writing a personal narrative, students can orally state a sentence that shows an understanding of the content vocabulary word *main idea*. An Idea Completion sentence can include words or phrases, such as *summary of a story*, that guides students to use the word appropriately. An example of a sentence starter can be the following:

- Writers include a *main idea* or a *summary of a story* because ________.

This Idea Completion sentence which hints that a main idea is a summary of a story can help students to orally use vocabulary in the right context.

How Does It Work?

1. Decide which specialized content and/or general academic vocabulary words are the focus of the lesson.
2. Create an Idea Completion sentence for each vocabulary word. Be sure to use clue words in the sentence to help students complete them appropriately. Write the Idea Completion sentences on the board.
3. Show students the first sentence and read it aloud. Model how you might complete the sentence orally, using a think-aloud strategy to share what words or clues in the sentence provide ideas for completing the sentence appropriately.
4. Continue to discuss the vocabulary word by having students orally share additional ideas for completing the sentence.
5. Write the next Idea Completion sentence on the board, model how to complete it, and then ask students to share ideas for completing it.
6. Repeat this process with the remaining vocabulary words.
7. Conclude the strategy by asking students how using the Idea Completion sentences helped them better understand the meaning of each word.

Differentiation

English language support—Preteach this strategy to a small group of students. Write appropriately leveled Idea Completion sentences on the board. Guide students in restating the entire sentence.

Below-level students—Show students how to complete Idea Completion sentences for vocabulary study. Start with vocabulary words that are familiar to them and write sentence starters for those words. Then show students that the sentences contain clues to help them understand the words.

Above-level students—Have students work in pairs to create Idea Completion sentences for each other. Students can use the same words and then compare their sentences. Or, they can each choose a different vocabulary word and write a sentence starter to share with a partner.

Strategy Category:

Developing Word Consciousness

Materials

- chart paper
- markers
- sticky notes (10 per group of students)
- piece of text related to lesson focus

Ten Important Words

What Is It?

The Ten Important Words strategy (Yopp, Yopp, and Bishop 2009) helps build students' awareness of the vocabulary words that they encounter. Students are instructed to find important words, or words essential to understanding a text. Those important words are then gathered, sorted, and graphed. After a discussion about the important words, students can include some of those words in a written or oral summary of the text.

When and Why Do I Use It?

Ten Important Words should be used during a lesson or unit as a strategy for reinforcing key terms. This strategy can be effective with both general academic and specialized content words. This strategy enhances students' reading comprehension skills as they scan a text and look for words related to the main idea. Additionally, students gain new understandings about vocabulary words and how they are used in context.

Example

For a science lesson on the water cycle, the following are 10 important words students can identify as important within their texts:

- accumulation
- condensation
- cumulonimbus
- droplets
- ecosystem
- evaporation
- precipitation
- rain
- transpiration
- water cycle

From the important words selected, students can then work in pairs to generate sentences that summarize the text.

How Does It Work?

1. To prepare for the strategy, choose a text or passage for students to read. This text should include essential vocabulary words related to the topic of study.
2. Share the text with students. Provide them with a short summary of the text. Decide whether students will read in pairs or in small groups.
3. Explain the directions for the activity. Tell students that when they are finished reading, they will identify ten important words in the text. They will use sticky notes to mark words and will then write the ten words on the sticky notes.
4. Distribute 10 sticky notes to each pair or small group. Then give students time to read in pairs or groups and write one word on each sticky note.
5. As a whole class, create a bar graph of the words that students chose. Use a large sheet of chart paper to make the graph. Each column should represent a different word. Have each pair put its sticky notes in the appropriate place on the bar graph. The sticky notes will create the bars on the graph.
6. Once all words are graphed, ask students to look at the results. Ask, "Which words were chosen the most? Why are these words important? What do they mean in this text? Which words were chosen the least? Why do you think fewer students chose these words?"
7. Work as a group to write a few sentences that summarize the text. Write the sentences on the chart.
8. Allow time for students to copy the summary sentences onto their paper or create their own summaries.
9. In conclusion, ask students how choosing ten important words, graphing them, and writing summaries helped them to better understand the words and ideas related to the text.

Differentiation

English language support—Read the text to students in a small group. Guide students in identifying ten important words. Then continue to work in a small group to develop a summary sentence that uses two or three of the words.

Below-level students—Read the text to students in a small group. Guide students in identifying the first four words. Continue to work in a small group to develop a summary sentence that uses the words.

Above-level students—While the class is working, ask students to work in pairs to sort words into categories. Then, have students share their ideas about the categories and each of their corresponding words.

Strategy Category:

Developing Word Consciousness

Materials

- chart paper
- markers
- piece of text related to lesson focus

Word Hunt

What Is It?

The Word Hunt strategy (Yopp, Yopp, and Bishop 2009) gives students an opportunity to locate word parts that they are studying in the world around them. Students record the word, its definition, and the location in which it was found. Word Hunt can be a fun, motivating way to help build student interest in interaction with vocabulary. Extensions of this strategy include sorting and/or graphing the word parts that students find to prompt further discussion and to deepen understanding of new vocabulary.

When and Why Do I Use It?

The Word Hunt strategy should be used either during or at the conclusion of a lesson or unit. This strategy should be used with general academic or specialized content words that include word parts that students have already learned. This strategy focuses on vocabulary words and word parts in context so that students can learn how word parts provide information about unfamiliar words and their definitions.

Example

For a language arts lesson on autobiographies, a student's completed chart can look like the following:

Word	Word Part	Definition	Where It Was Found
autobiography	*auto-*	a book about someone's life, written by the person	language arts textbook
biography	*bio-*	a book about someone's life, written by someone else	magazine
memoir	*mem-*	a narrative written from personal experiences	newspaper

How Does It Work?

1. Before using this strategy, decide which vocabulary words to use. You can use specialized content and/or general academic words, but the words should include word parts that have already been taught to students.
2. Decide how students will record the results of the Word Hunts. Students can write the word parts on sheets of paper or in their journals. Students should include the entire word, the word part, the definition, and where it was found.
3. To begin, explain to students that they are going on a Word Hunt. Share the word parts and example words that will be the focus of this activity. Ask students if they need clarification on any of the words or word-part meanings. Encourage other students to share definitions or examples.
4. Explain to students how to complete this activity. Challenge them to find examples of the words or related word parts. They may find them in trade books, textbooks, the environmental print around the classroom, or their homes. Students will record what they find on a chart. Share with students the amount of time in which they will conduct the Word Hunt. **Note:** A reading passage is included for the lessons in this resource that integrate this strategy.
5. Have students share their findings with the rest of the class. Ask them to discuss each word, word part, definition, and where the word was found. Record their contributions on chart paper.
6. Decide how to extend this strategy for further discussion and review. Some examples could include asking students as a group to review the class findings, and sort or graph the words together, challenging students to use the words in a paragraph or short story, or having students find additional words that use the same word parts.
7. In conclusion, ask students how hunting for words and word parts helped them better understand new vocabulary. Let students discuss this in pairs first before discussing it as a whole group.

Differentiation

English language support—Choose three word parts from the vocabulary list for the activity. Review with students examples of words that include the same word parts. Discuss definitions and common uses of the word parts and the words.

Below-level students—Ask students to each share a word part and discuss a connection that they have to it or how they think the word part might be used appropriately.

Above-level students—Have students work as a group and use the words that they find to create a story. Have them choose three words and put them together to draft a short paragraph or act out a scene.

Strategy Category:

Teaching Words

Materials

- chart paper
- markers

Vocabulary Diagram

What Is It?

The Vocabulary Diagram strategy (Yopp, Yopp, and Bishop 2009) enables students to examine individual words according to different categories. Students look at a given word and identify its synonyms and antonyms, other forms of the word, and a sentence from their reading that uses the word. Then students record this information, draw a picture that represents the word, and create an original sentence that uses the word.

When and Why Do I Use It?

A Vocabulary Diagram should be used at the beginning of a lesson or unit. This strategy should be used with a dynamic word that is essential to understanding the lesson or unit. This word should be a specialized content word that may be new for students. Analyzing a single word through different vocabulary categories makes it possible for students to recognize and decode a greater number of unknown words during reading and promotes better long-term retention of vocabulary words.

Example

For a social studies lesson on people who have made a significant contribution in the field of transportation, a vocabulary word that can be incorporated into the diagram can be *transportation*. The example to the left shows a completed Vocabulary Diagram integrating the word *transportation*.

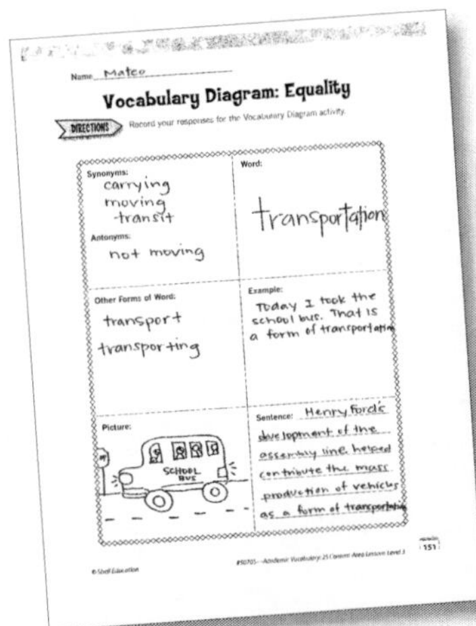

Name: Mateo

Vocabulary Diagram: Equality

DIRECTIONS Record your responses for the Vocabulary Diagram activity.

Synonyms: carrying, moving, transit Antonyms: not moving	Word: transportation
Other Forms of Word: transport, transporting	Example: Today I took the school bus. That is a form of transportation
Picture: SCHOOL BUS	Sentence: Henry Ford's development of the assembly line helped contribute the mass production of vehicles as a form of transportation

© Shell Education #50705—Academic Vocabulary: 25 Content-Area Lessons Level 3 151

How Does It Work?

1. Before using this strategy, decide which vocabulary word to use. Use a specialized content word that may be unfamiliar to students. This word should be one that is found within the text and is essential to understanding.
2. To prepare, create a Vocabulary Diagram on a sheet of chart paper.
3. Tell students that they will analyze a vocabulary word that is important to the lesson. Write the word on the board. Then read the text or trade book that contains the selected word.
4. Explain to students how to complete the diagram. Point out and explain each part of the diagram. Then write the selected word in the appropriate area on the chart. Ask students to repeat the sentence from the text and write it in the corresponding area on the chart.
5. Tell students that they will work as a class to discuss the word and fill in the remaining parts of the diagram. Complete all of the parts except for the drawing.
6. Allow students to share other forms of the word. Then create an original sentence that uses the word.
7. When the diagram is complete, ask students to work in pairs to create a picture that represents the word. Allow students to share their pictures with the class.
8. In conclusion, talk with students about the importance of knowing a word's synonyms and antonyms, finding other forms of the word, being able to use the word in an original sentence, and drawing a picture to remember the word. Ask students to discuss their responses.

Differentiation

English language support—Work with a small group of students. Focus on drawing a visual for the word to build students' background knowledge. When appropriate, have students act out the word to solidify their understanding.

Below-level students—Work with a small group of students to complete portions of the diagram. Discuss familiar synonyms for the word to build students' background knowledge.

Above-level students—Allow students to further investigate their selected word. Encourage them to create their own Vocabulary Diagram with different categories.

Strategy Category:

Teaching Words

Materials

- index cards

Content Links

What Is It?

Content Links (Yopp, Yopp, and Bishop 2009) is a strategy that helps students see how vocabulary words are connected to each other. This strategy begins with the teacher creating a word list related to the unit. Then each student takes a card with a vocabulary word written on it, and the class mingles. Each student finds another student who has a vocabulary word that can be linked to his or her word in some way.

When and Why Do I Use It?

Content Links should be used either during or at the conclusion of a lesson or unit as a strategy for working with related vocabulary words. This strategy should be used with general academic or specialized content vocabulary words that students have already learned. This strategy allows students to have meaningful conversations with their peers about vocabulary and discuss relationships between words. Because there is no right answer, students make their own decisions about linked words and their thinking with others.

Example

For a science lesson on the classification of living things, the following word pairs can be created:

insect	spider
mammal	monkey
carnivore	shark
herbivore	horse
reptile	lizard
producer	plants
omnivore	human
invertebrate	squid

How Does It Work?

1. Before using this strategy, decide which vocabulary words to use. Although the strategy is more appropriate for specialized content words, general academic words can be used as well. Students should have learned these words prior to this activity.

2. Create Content Links word cards. Write each word on its own index card. If possible, have enough words so that each student in the class has his or her own word.

3. Hold up each word card and read the words aloud. Choose a few words to reread. As a class, clap as each syllable is said aloud. Ask students if they need clarification on any of the words' meanings. Take time to discuss words as needed. If necessary, show pictures, use gestures, or use the words in context.

4. Explain to students how to complete the activity. Tell students that they will get into pairs to make links, or matches, between two vocabulary words. Once in pairs, students will discuss how the words are related. Then students will share their ideas with the class. Model this by holding up two word cards that have words that can be linked. Read the words, explain their meanings, and tell how the words are linked. Emphasize that the words do not have to match exactly; they simply must be connected in some way.

5. Distribute one word card to each student. Then give students time to mingle. Students should find links for their vocabulary words.

6. Ask students to stand together with their partners and form a circle around the room. **Note:** There is a chance that some students will find no match.

7. Have each pair discuss their words, the definitions, and how the words are connected. If some students found no match, ask them to explain why those words were difficult to relate to other words.

8. In conclusion, ask students how making connections between vocabulary words has helped them better understand those words.

Differentiation

English language support—Make sure that students understand what the selected words mean. Modify the word cards by adding a simple sketch or visual representation of each word's meaning.

Below-level students—Have students echo-read each word on cards. Review the definition and explanation of each word. Use pictures, sketches, or gestures whenever possible to communicate the words' meanings.

Above-level students—After students have linked pairs of words, have pairs link their words to those of other pairs of students. Ask the group of students to explain how they linked the four words.

Introduction

Strategy Category:

Independent Word Learning

Materials

- chart paper
- markers

Vocabulary Journal

What Is It?

The Vocabulary Journal strategy offers students a variety of ways to work with important terms and concepts. Students can use their journals to make personal connections to words, write about word-learning strategies, write sentences or short stories using vocabulary words, or jot down words that are interesting and unique. Vocabulary Journals can be used with students of all ages and academic levels. Modify the requirements of the Vocabulary Journals to fit the needs of your students. For example, younger students' journal entries may include drawings; older students' entries might record graphic organizers related to their word study.

When and Why Do I Use It?

Vocabulary Journals can be used throughout a unit of study to provide a place for students to reflect on and record information about vocabulary words. These journals can be used with both specialized content and general academic words.

Example

For a mathematics lesson on adding decimals, a specialized content vocabulary word can be *decimal*. The example to the left shows a completed Vocabulary Journal entry for the word *decimal*.

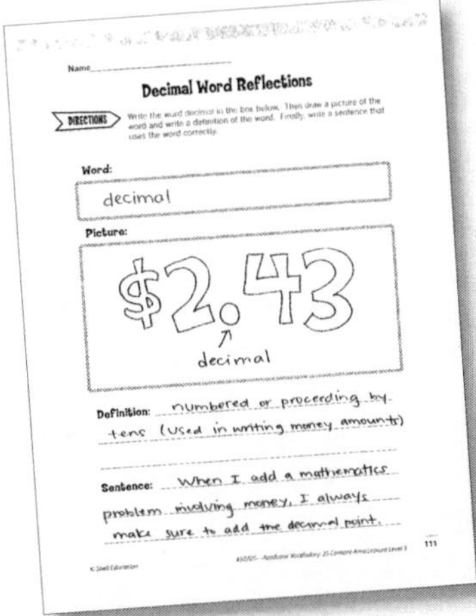

Name________

Decimal Word Reflections

DIRECTIONS Write the word decimal in the box below. Then draw a picture of the word and write a definition of the word. Finally, write a sentence that uses the word correctly.

Word: decimal

Picture:

Definition: numbered or proceeding by tens (used in writing money amounts)

Sentence: When I add a mathematics problem involving money, I always make sure to add the decimal point.

111

How Does It Work?

1. Before using this strategy, decide which vocabulary words are key to the lesson and/or unit.
2. Before introducing this strategy, create a Vocabulary Journal for each student. Decide how to integrate them into each lesson and unit. For example, students may be asked to record one predetermined word (a key concept for the lesson) in their journals at the conclusion of each lesson.
3. Explain to students that the journals are a place for them to reflect on vocabulary words. This can be done in a variety of ways:
   - Record new vocabulary words and their student-friendly definitions. Include related words or synonyms and antonyms.
   - Write a vocabulary word and then create a visual aid related to it. This may be as simple as an illustration or as complex as a chart, graphic organizer, or diagram.
   - Use the vocabulary words appropriately in sentences.
   - Write about vocabulary strategies that have been tried and describe what worked best.
   - Explain any personal connections to vocabulary words or related ideas.
4. Introduce the strategy by modeling the Vocabulary Journal entry. Re-create the Vocabulary Journal entry on a sheet of chart paper. At the conclusion of a lesson, show students how to create a journal entry for a selected vocabulary word.
5. Ask students to take out their Vocabulary Journals. Have each student create an entry for another selected word from the lesson.
6. Vocabulary Journals can be periodically shared with the class. In addition, the teacher can occasionally write to students in their journals and create an ongoing dialogue with them about vocabulary. This would give you a chance to offer feedback about their work, share ideas about new vocabulary learning strategies, or suggest new sources for related vocabulary.

Differentiation

English language support—Have students share ideas from their journals in small groups. This gives them a chance to discuss vocabulary and to practice including it in their oral language.

Below-level students—Let students' journal entries be appropriate for their skill level. This may mean students write about fewer words, write shorter examples, or choose vocabulary that is appropriate for them.

Above-level students—Challenge students to use journals to extend their knowledge of words. Try to design assignments with more complex vocabulary and/or related activities.

Strategy Category:

Independent Word Learning

Materials

- none

Clue Hunt

What Is It?

Context refers to the clues authors include before and after vocabulary to aid readers in understanding new terms. These clues may be direct or indirect, and deciphering them is not always easy. Yet if students can discern some level of meaning for new vocabulary based on other information presented in the text, reading comprehension and vocabulary knowledge will be enhanced. In the Clue Hunt strategy (Yopp, Yopp, and Bishop 2009), students have an engaging and authentic reason for identifying and using context clues found in texts—a "scavenger hunt" for context clues in classroom reading materials.

When and Why Do I Use It?

The Clue Hunt strategy should be introduced only after students have a solid understanding of the various types of context clues. The Clue Hunt can then be repeated throughout the school year. Students are exposed to many vocabulary words as they read content area text. Therefore, it is important that they use context to help determine the meaning of unfamiliar words. This strategy can be effective with both specialized content and general academic words.

Example

For a language arts lesson on literary devices, students' Clue Hunt table might look like this:

Words	Context Clues in Text
interpret	Readers must often *interpret*, or understand the meaning behind, what a character does and says.
simile	The poet decided to include a *simile*. This comparison of two things, which includes the words *like* or *as* helps describe the differences between them.
incorporate	Authors *incorporate* certain literary devices to help enhance the narrative. Leaving these interesting details out makes a story weaker.

How Does It Work?

1. Before using this strategy, identify key vocabulary words in the text. These can be specialized content or general academic words.
2. Look at the text to identify the context clues provided by the author(s) for each word you have chosen:
   - **Direct Definitions:** Authors often put a direct definition of a vocabulary word within the sentence. The word meaning is explained clearly and directly and can often be identified by a comma or a set of commas.
   - **Synonyms:** Authors may include a synonym near an unfamiliar word to help cue the reader about its definition.
   - **Antonyms:** Just as synonyms provide linguistic context clues, antonyms also help students find meaning in new words.
   - **Sentence/Paragraph:** It is important for students to learn that context clues are not always placed within the same sentence as the unfamiliar vocabulary word. Additional sentences and entire paragraphs may need to be examined for clues. Students should remember that authors can be quite purposeful with their word choices and that each word should be considered as part of a larger body of text meant to convey a certain idea or concept.
3. Read the text as planned during the lesson. Ask students to locate the selected words. Guide students to identify and analyze the context clues in the text.
4. After students have finished reading the text and recording the vocabulary words and context clues, review students' findings. Have students label the clues and/or sort them by type.
5. After introducing the strategy, provide multiple opportunities for students to conduct Clue Hunts with other words and other pieces of text.
6. To conclude, ask students how using context clues can help them understand the unfamiliar words that they read.

Differentiation

English language support—While pairs of students read the text, work with a small group. Read the text to them and point out important information to build background knowledge.

Below-level students—Provide students with clear, explicit examples of each type of context clue. Write these on a sheet of chart paper for students' reference. Guide students in using the examples to identify and sort the clues found in the selected text.

Above-level students—Ask students to share their own techniques for using context to build word knowledge. They might have methods that they use while reading that could benefit other students in the class.

Overview of Assessment

Personal Examples

The Personal Examples assessment asks students to connect what they know about learned vocabulary words with their own personal experiences and backgrounds. These connections demonstrate the level of students' vocabulary knowledge. This format also requires students to show deeper and more comprehensive knowledge of a new word because they need to apply their knowledge of the word to a context that may be new or different from what was discussed in class.

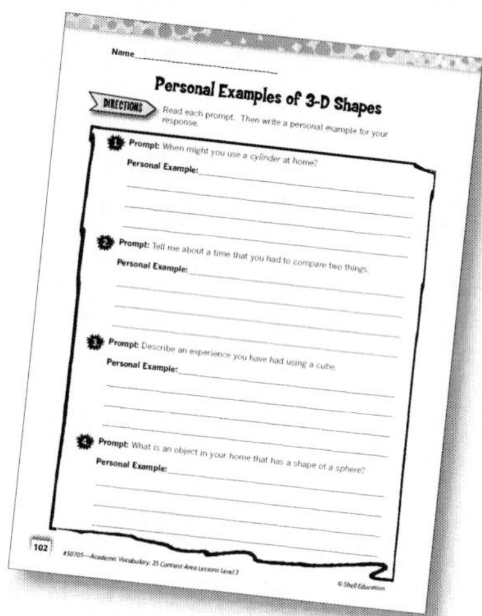
Name____________________

Personal Examples of 3-D Shapes

DIRECTIONS Read each prompt. Then write a personal example for your response.

1. **Prompt:** When might you use a *cylinder* at home?
   Personal Example: ____________________
2. **Prompt:** Tell me about a time that you had to *compare* two things.
   Personal Example: ____________________
3. **Prompt:** Describe an experience you have had using a *cube*.
   Personal Example: ____________________
4. **Prompt:** What is an object in your home that has a shape of a *sphere*?
   Personal Example: ____________________

102 #50705—Academic Vocabulary: 25 Content-Area Lessons Level 3 © Shell Education

Context Interpretation

Context Interpretation assesses how well students are able to use new vocabulary words within an appropriate context. Students read a context statement that uses the vocabulary word and a question related to that statement. Students then write a response to the question based on the context statement.

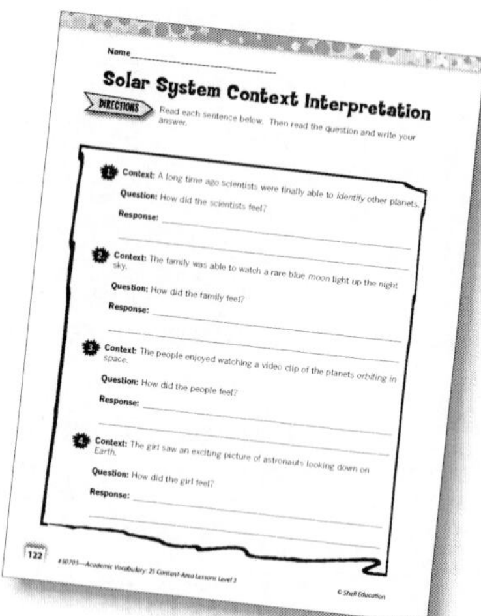
Name____________________

Solar System Context Interpretation

DIRECTIONS Read each sentence below. Then read the question and write your answer.

1. **Context:** A long time ago scientists were finally able to *identify* other planets.
   Question: How did the scientists feel?
   Response: ____________________
2. **Context:** The family was able to watch a rare blue *moon* light up the night sky.
   Question: How did the family feel?
   Response: ____________________
3. **Context:** The people enjoyed watching a video clip of the planets *orbiting in space*.
   Question: How did the people feel?
   Response: ____________________
4. **Context:** The girl saw an exciting picture of astronauts looking down on *Earth*.
   Question: How did the girl feel?
   Response: ____________________

122 #50705—Academic Vocabulary: 25 Content-Area Lessons Level 3 © Shell Education

Context Completion

Another assessment that requires students to use context as they consider learned vocabulary is the Context Completion activity. Students must use what they know about vocabulary to complete sentence frames, either orally or in writing. These Context Completion sentences may also encourage students to use academic language patterns as they complete semantically correct statements.

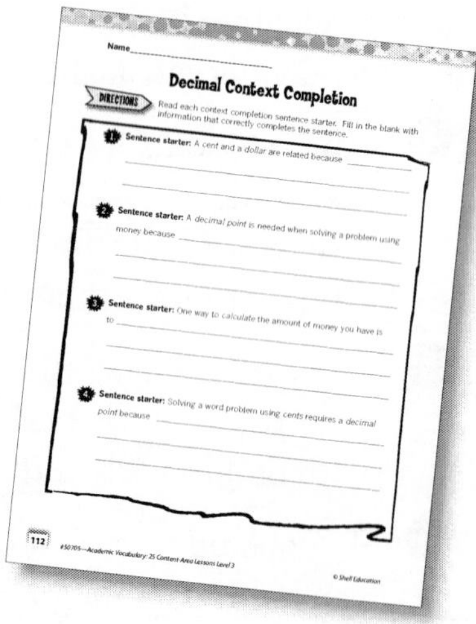
Name____________________

Decimal Context Completion

DIRECTIONS Read each context completion sentence starter. Fill in the blank with information that correctly completes the sentence.

1. **Sentence starter:** A *cent* and a *dollar* are related because ____________________
2. **Sentence starter:** A *decimal point* is needed when solving a problem using money because ____________________
3. **Sentence starter:** One way to *calculate* the amount of money you have is to ____________________
4. **Sentence starter:** Solving a word problem using *cents* requires a *decimal point* because ____________________

112 #50705—Academic Vocabulary: 25 Content-Area Lessons Level 3 © Shell Education

Overview of Assessment *(cont.)*

Word Translations

The Word Translations assessment gives students an opportunity to consider academic language and how it relates to a more informal and casual style of communicating. This assessment provides an opportunity for students to use focus vocabulary within the structure of formal language patterns. Meanwhile, students are also capable of showing their understanding of the more basic meanings behind words and their uses.

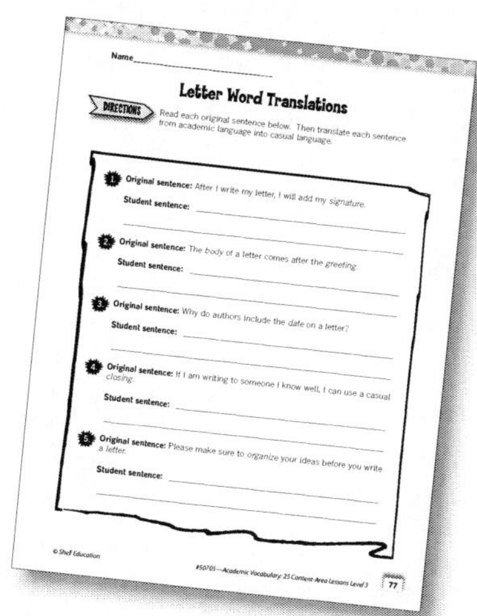

Name____________________

Letter Word Translations

DIRECTIONS Read each original sentence below. Then translate each sentence from academic language into casual language.

1. **Original sentence:** After I write my letter, I will add my *signature.*
   Student sentence: ____________________
2. **Original sentence:** The *body* of a letter comes after the *greeting.*
   Student sentence: ____________________
3. **Original sentence:** Why do authors include the *date* on a letter?
   Student sentence: ____________________
4. **Original sentence:** If I am writing to someone I know well, I can use a casual *closing.*
   Student sentence: ____________________
5. **Original sentence:** Please make sure to *organize* your ideas before you write a *letter.*
   Student sentence: ____________________

© Shell Education #50705—Academic Vocabulary: 25 Content-Area Lessons Level 3 77

Yes-No-Why?

The Yes-No-Why? assessment format provides students with a sentence that includes focus vocabulary. The students read a sentence that includes one or more learned vocabulary words. They must then evaluate whether the sentence makes sense and explain their reasoning in a short response of one or more sentences. Students must consider what they know about a word's definition and decide whether the real-world application is appropriate. This higher-level thinking challenges students to analyze new vocabulary words and their proper uses.

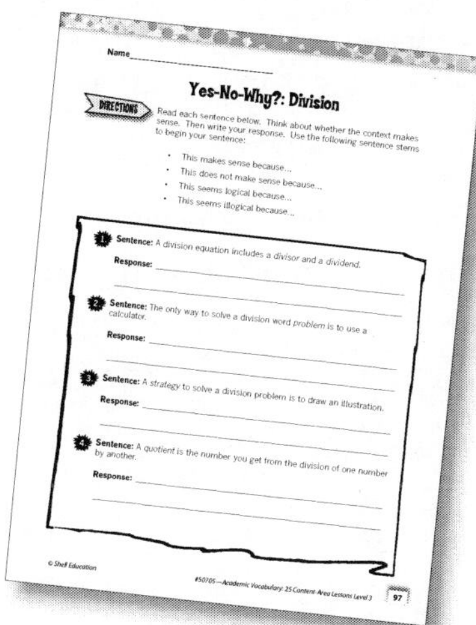

Name____________________

Yes-No-Why?: Division

DIRECTIONS Read each sentence below. Think about whether the context makes sense. Then write your response. Use the following sentence stems to begin your sentence:

- This makes sense because...
- This does not make sense because...
- This seems logical because...
- This seems illogical because...

1. **Sentence:** A division equation includes a *divisor* and a *dividend.*
   Response: ____________________
2. **Sentence:** The only way to solve a division word *problem* is to use a calculator.
   Response: ____________________
3. **Sentence:** A *strategy* to solve a division problem is to draw an illustration.
   Response: ____________________
4. **Sentence:** A *quotient* is the number you get from the division of one number by another.
   Response: ____________________

© Shell Education #50705—Academic Vocabulary: 25 Content-Area Lessons Level 3 97

Show You Know

The Show You Know assessment tool requires students to show their word knowledge by using written vocabulary appropriately and in context. Students read a pair of words and then write their responses based on how the pair of words connect to the lesson. Students' responses show the connections they made between vocabulary words. Additionally, this assessment may allow students to integrate academic language patterns into their writing.

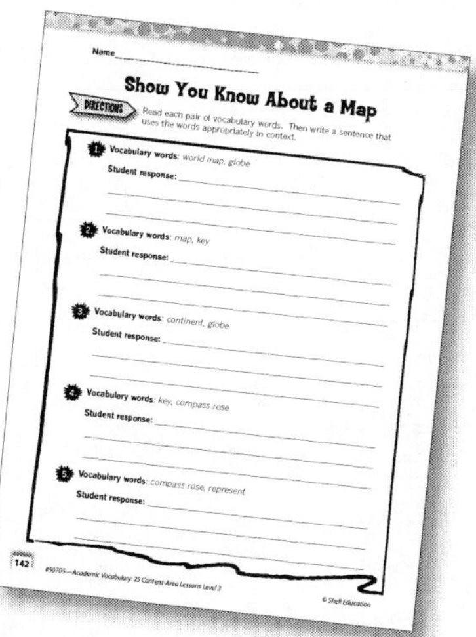

Name____________________

Show You Know About a Map

DIRECTIONS Read each pair of vocabulary words. Then write a sentence that uses the words appropriately in context.

1. **Vocabulary words**: *world map, globe*
   Student response: ____________________
2. **Vocabulary words**: *map, key*
   Student response: ____________________
3. **Vocabulary words**: *continent, globe*
   Student response: ____________________
4. **Vocabulary words**: *key, compass rose*
   Student response: ____________________
5. **Vocabulary words**: *compass rose, represent*
   Student response: ____________________

142 #50705—Academic Vocabulary: 25 Content-Area Lessons Level 3 © Shell Education

Standards Correlations

Shell Education is committed to producing educational materials that are research and standards based. In this effort, we have correlated all of our products to the academic standards of all 50 United States, the District of Columbia, the Department of Defense Dependent Schools, and all Canadian provinces. We have also correlated to the Common Core State Standards.

How to Find Standards Correlations

To print a customized correlation report of this product for your state, visit our website at **http://www.shelleducation.com** and follow the on-screen directions. If you require assistance in printing correlation reports, please contact Customer Service at 1-877-777-3450.

Purpose and Intent of Standards

Legislation mandates that all states adopt academic standards that identify the skills students will learn in kindergarten through grade twelve. Many states also have standards for Pre-K. This same legislation sets requirements to ensure the standards are detailed and comprehensive.

Standards are designed to focus instruction and guide adoption of curricula. Standards are statements that describe the criteria necessary for students to meet specific academic goals. They define the knowledge, skills, and content students should acquire at each level. Standards are also used to develop standardized tests to evaluate students' academic progress. Teachers are required to demonstrate how their lessons meet state standards. State standards are used in the development of all of our products, so educators can be assured they meet the academic requirements of each state.

McREL Compendium

We use the Mid-continent Research for Education and Learning (McREL) Compendium to create standards correlations. Each year, McREL analyzes state standards and revises the compendium. By following this procedure, McREL is able to produce a general compilation of national standards. Each lesson in this product is based on one or more McREL standards. The chart on the following pages lists each standard taught in this product and the page number(s) for the corresponding lessons.

TESOL Standards

The lessons in this book promote English language development for English language learners. The standards listed on the following pages support the language objectives presented throughout the lessons.

Correlation to McREL Standards

The main focus of the lessons presented in *Academic Vocabulary: 25 Content-Area Lessons* is to promote the development of academic vocabulary. The chart below and on the following page lists standards correlated to the lessons in this book.

Language Arts Standards	Page(s)
1.6—Uses strategies to write for a variety for purposes	68, 78
1.7—Writes expository compositions	78
1.8—Writes narrative accounts, such as poems and stories	63
1.12—Writes personal letters	73
2.1—Uses descriptive and precise language that clarifies and enhances ideas	68
5.7—Understands level-appropriate sight words and vocabulary	38, 43, 48, 53, 58, 93, 103, 148, 153
6.0—Uses skills and strategies to read a variety of literary texts	118
6.1—Reads a variety of literary passages and texts	38, 48, 53, 58
6.2—Knows the defining characteristics and structural elements of a variety of literary genres	83
7.1—Reads a variety of informational texts	43
8.3—Responds to questions and comments	88, 143
8.6—Uses level-appropriate vocabulary in speech	63, 73, 83, 98, 108, 113, 123, 128, 133, 138, 153, 158

Mathematics Standards	Page(s)
2.5—Understands the concepts related to fractions and decimals	103
3.1—Multiplies and divides whole numbers	93
3.7—Understands the properties of and the relationships among addition, subtraction, multiplication, and division	88
3.8—Solves word problems and real-world problems involving number operations, including those that specify units	108
5.1—Knows basic geometric language for describing and naming shapes	98

Correlation to McREL Standards *(cont.)*

Science Standards	Page(s)
1.1—Knows that water exists in the air in different forms and changes from one form to another through various processes	113
3.2—Knows that Earth is one of several planets that orbit the sun and that the moon orbits Earth	118
5.2—Knows that living organisms have distinct structures and body systems that serve specific functions in growth, survival, and reproduction	123
8.1—Knows that matter has different states and that each state has distinct physical properties	128
12.3—Plans and conducts simple investigations	133

Social Studies Standards	Page(s)
1.1—Knows the basic elements of maps and globes	138
2.0—Knows the location of places, geographic features, and patterns of the environment	143
4.3—Understands how people over the last 200 years have continued to struggle to bring to all groups in American society the liberties and equality promised in the basic principles of American democracy	148
8.0—Understands major discoveries in science and the major scientists and inventors responsible for them	153
8.7—Understands the development of extensive road systems	158

Correlation to TESOL Standards

The main focus of the lessons presented in *Academic Vocabulary: 25 Content-Area Lessons* is to promote the development of academic vocabulary. The standards listed below support the language objectives presented throughout the lessons.

TESOL Standards	Page(s)
1.3—To use English to communicate in social settings: Students will use learning strategies to extend their communicative competence	113
2.2—To use English to achieve academically in all content areas: Students will use English to obtain, process, construct, and provide subject-matter information in spoken and written form	68, 78, 98, 118, 123, 128, 133, 143, 148, 153, 158,
2.3—To use English to achieve academically in all content areas: Students will use appropriate learning strategies to construct and apply academic knowledge	38, 43, 48, 53, 58, 63, 73, 83, 88, 93, 103, 108, 138

Life Stories

Featured Academic Vocabulary Strategies

- **Alike and Different:** Developing Oral Language (page 16)
- **Word Hunt:** Developing Word Consciousness (page 22)

Standards

- **McREL:** Students will read a variety of literary passages and texts.
- **McREL:** Students will understand level-appropriate sight words and vocabulary.
- **TESOL:** Students will use appropriate learning strategies to construct and apply academic knowledge.

Materials

- chart paper
- marker
- *The World According to Roald Dahl* (page 40)
- *Related Words* (page 41)
- *Yes-No-Why?: Autobiography and Biography* (page 42)

Focus Vocabulary Words	
Specialized Content Vocabulary	**General Academic Vocabulary**
autobiography biography chronology	retell

Procedure

1. Write the vocabulary pair *biography* and *autobiography* on the board. Use the **Alike and Different** strategy (page 16) to help students make connections among the words and deepen their understanding of the vocabulary.
2. Ask students to think about what they know about each of these words. Then ask students to discuss how these words are similar and different. Record students' responses on a sheet of chart paper using a two-columned chart.
3. Use the **Word Hunt** strategy (page 22) to further examine the word parts that are included in the vocabulary words *autobiography* and *biography*. The following is an example of the word parts found in *autobiography* and *biography*:

Word	Word Part	Definition	Examples
autobiography	*auto-*	self	autograph
	bio-	life	biology
	graph-	writing	telegraph
biography	*bio-*	life	biology
	graph-	writing	telegraph

Procedure *(cont.)*

4. Distribute copies of the *The World According to Roald Dahl* reading passage (page 40) to students. Read the passage aloud to students. Have them talk in pairs about how they know that this is an example of a *biography*. Discuss this as a group, referencing some of the vocabulary words. For example, students can be asked, "What do you notice about the *chronology* of this passage? How can you tell this is a *biography*?"

5. Distribute copies of the *Related Words* activity sheet (page 41) to students. Explain that they will be doing a word hunt for the words *biography* and *autobiography* using *The World According to Roald Dahl* reading passage. Have students *retell* the passage to a partner. When students are finished, give them time to write about the similiarities and differences between a *biography* and an *autobiography*.

6. Distribute copies of the *Yes-No-Why?: Autobiography and Biography* assessment sheet (page 42) to students. Have students complete the assessment individually as a way to evaluate whether students can recognize if sentences that use the new vocabulary words make sense or not.

Differentiation

English language support—Share some Roald Dahl books with students and briefly summarize the plots of each book. Encourage students to share their thoughts on Roald Dahl.

Below-level students—Refer students back to the passage to find concrete examples of chronological order. Discuss how a reader knows this biography is written in the order in which it happened.

Above-level students—Encourage students to further research Roald Dahl to expand on the biography reading passage.

Name________________________________

The World According to Roald Dahl

DIRECTIONS Read the passage. Then answer the questions below.

Roald Dahl is one of the most popular children's authors of all time. Many authors have written biographies about him. He is best known for writing silly, imaginative stories with vivid characters. *Charlie and the Chocolate Factory, James and the Giant Peach, and Matilda* are just some of his most famous stories.

Roald Dahl was born on September 13, 1916. As a boy, he loved books and he loved to write. He even began to write a diary at the age of eight! His diary became his autobiography. Many of Roald's memories of childhood can be found in his stories. For example, many of his ideas for *Charlie and the Chocolate Factory* were taken from his own experiences as a child wanting some candy.

Roald Dahl died in 1990. His stories still delight kids all over the world because of his creativity. Roald Dahl's books continue to be favorites among many children.

1. What are some stories Roald Dahl wrote?

____

____

2. Why do you think many people enjoy Roald Dahl's stories?

____

____

Name________________________________

Related Words

DIRECTIONS Read *The World According to Roald Dahl*. When you are done reading, go back and do a Word Hunt for the words *autobiography* and *biography*. Use this page to record the word part and definition to your findings.

Word	Word Part	Definition
autobiography		
biography		

DIRECTIONS Look at your findings above. What is similar about an *autobiography* and a *biography*? What is different?

____

____

____

____

____

____

____

Name________________________________

Yes-No-Why?: Autobiography and Biography

DIRECTIONS Read each sentence below. Think about whether the context makes sense. Then write your response. Use the following sentence stems to begin your sentence:

- This makes sense because...
- This does not make sense because...
- This seems logical because...
- This seems illogical because...

1. **Sentence**: The easiest way to *retell* a story about a person's life is to summarize the events in *chronological* order.

   Response: ____

   ____

   ____

2. **Sentence:** An *autobiography* always has only one character in it.

   Response: ____

   ____

   ____

3. **Sentence:** A *biography* is written by the person about whom it is about.

   Response: ____

   ____

   ____

4. **Sentence:** Readers may best examine a person's life by reading an *autobiography*.

   Response: ____

   ____

   ____

Follow the Directions

Featured Academic Vocabulary Strategies

- **Have You Ever?:** Developing Oral Language (page 10)
- **Content Links:** Teaching Words (page 26)

Standards

- **McREL:** Students will read a variety of informational texts.
- **McREL:** Students will understand level-appropriate sight words and vocabulary.
- **TESOL:** Students will use appropriate learning strategies to construct and apply academic knowledge.

Materials

- newspaper
- chart paper
- marker
- *How to Make a Berry Good Smoothie* (page 45)
- index cards
- *Informational Links* (page 46)
- *Personal Examples on Directions* (page 47)

Focus Vocabulary Words	
Specialized Content Vocabulary	**General Academic Vocabulary**
informational text sequential	directions information list

Procedure

1. Begin the lesson by showing students a newspaper. Ask students to share what they know about newspapers. Guide students to the idea that a newspaper provides *information*. Explain that a newspaper is a type of *informational text*, and that informational text is text that provides you with information. Ask students to help you list other examples of informational texts. Write students' responses on the board.

2. Write the words *sequential*, *directions*, and *list* on the board. Discuss with students why these words are important to know when reading or writing informational texts. For example, you may say, "The *sequential* order of *information* in a recipe is very important."

3. As you continue to discuss these concepts, use the **Have You Ever?** strategy (page 10) to connect students' knowledge of the concepts to their own personal experiences. The following are some examples to include in the discussion:
   - When have you had to use a *list* of *directions*?
   - What types of *informational texts* are the most helpful or interesting to you?
   - Describe a time when you either read or wrote a *list*.
   - What helpful *information* have you read recently?

Procedure *(cont.)*

4. Distribute copies of the *How to Make a Berry Good Smoothie* reading passage (page 45) to students. Read the text aloud to students. Have students discuss in pairs what kind of text this is and how it is structured. Discuss this as a group, making sure to include some of the vocabulary students have learned. For example, students can be asked, "Why might the author have written this *information* in sequential order?"
5. Help facilitate a whole-class discussion about what students have learned about informational texts. Remind students of the vocabulary words from the lesson by writing them on the board. Then have students brainstorm additional words they learned that are related to this type of writing. End the list when there is one word for every student in the class.
6. Record the words on index cards and distribute one card to each student. Complete the **Content Links** strategy (page 26) with students to solidify their comprehension of the words necessary to understand the content of this lesson.
7. Distribute copies of the *Informational Links* activity sheet (page 46) to students. With the partner with whom they have linked, have students complete the first set of linking words together. Then have them find two additional partners to complete the rest of the activity sheet.
8. Distribute copies of the *Personal Examples on Directions* assessment sheet (page 47) to students. Have students complete the assessment individually to see whether they understand how to correctly apply their knowledge of new vocabulary to their own personal experiences.

Differentiation

English language support—Share different examples of informational texts that are written in a sequential order. Talk about the importance of writing and understanding the content in the order in which it is written. For example, what can happen if you do not follow a recipe in the correct order?

Below-level students—Modify the **Content Links** lesson by using fewer words and having students find only one or two different links. Discuss the links that students made and recorded.

Above-level students—Have students not only dicuss why their words link but also why cerain focus vocabulary words might not link. Have them share their ideas with the group.

Name________________________________

How to Make a Berry Good Smoothie

DIRECTIONS Read the recipe below.

Ingredients

$\frac{1}{2}$ cup of strawberries

$\frac{1}{2}$ cup of blueberries

$\frac{1}{2}$ cup of raspberries

1 banana

$\frac{1}{4}$ cup of vanilla yogurt

2 cups of ice

1 cup of orange juice

Materials Needed

measuring cups

cutting board

knife (adult use only)

blender

Wash all of the berries. Ask an adult to cut the stems off and to cut the strawberries in half.

Place the measurements of berries, vanilla yogurt, and orange juice into the blender.

Peel the banana. Break it into smaller pieces. Place the pieces in the blender.

Add the ice to the top of the mixture. Close the blender lid tightly and ask an adult to help you make sure the blender is ready.

Turn the blender on low. After a few seconds, turn it to high. Blend the ingredients until it is smooth.

Pour the smoothie into the glass. Enjoy!

Name_______________________________

Informational Links

DIRECTIONS Write the words you linked in the spaces below. Then write a short description of how and why the words are linked.

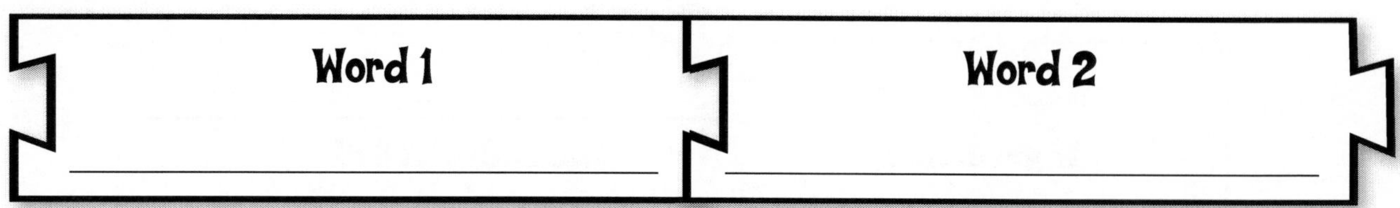

These words are linked because...

____

____

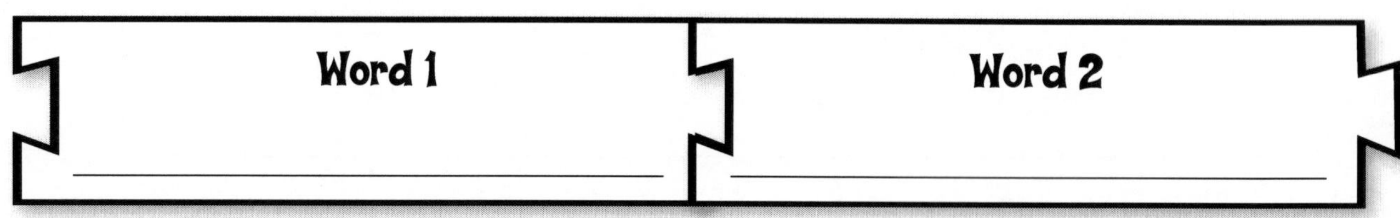

These words are linked because...

____

____

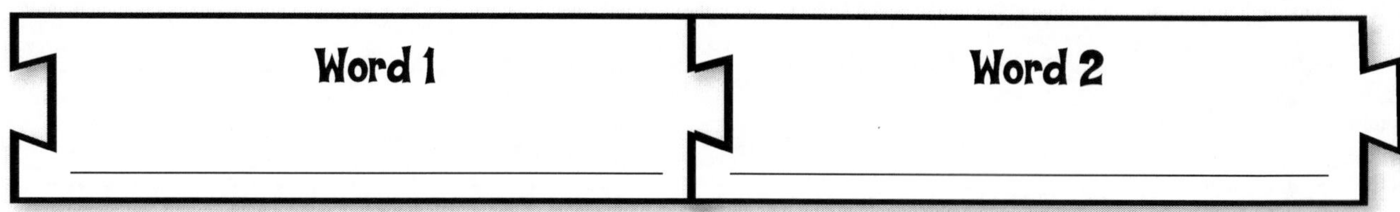

These words are linked because...

____

____

Name________________________________

Personal Examples on Directions

DIRECTIONS Read each prompt. Then write a personal example for your response.

1. **Prompt:** When might you need to read *directions*?

   Personal Example:________________________________

   ____

   ____

2. **Prompt:** Tell about a time when you wrote or read a *list*.

   Personal Example:________________________________

   ____

   ____

3. **Prompt:** Describe a time when something must happen in *sequential order*.

   Personal Example:________________________________

   ____

   ____

4. **Prompt:** Tell the main difference between *informational texts* and *fictional texts*.

   Personal Example:________________________________

   ____

   ____

A Fantasy World

Featured Academic Vocabulary Strategies

- **Idea Completions:** Developing Oral Language (page 18)
- **Vocabulary Journal:** Independent Word Learning (page 28)

Standards

- **McREL:** Students will read a variety of literary passages and texts.
- **McREL:** Students will understand level-appropriate sight words and vocabulary.
- **TESOL:** Students will use appropriate learning strategies to construct and apply academic knowledge.

Materials

- pictures depicting fantasy and real life
- chart paper
- marker
- *The Rock* (page 50)
- *Elements of a Fantasy Story* (page 51)
- *Fantasy Context Interpretation* (page 52)

Focus Vocabulary Words	
Specialized Content Vocabulary	**General Academic Vocabulary**
fantasy foreshadow plot	predict story

Procedure

1. Tell students that today they will be learning about *fantasy*. Explain that they will be seeing pictures depicting an image that can be fantasy or it can be real. Show the images to students to activate prior knowledge.
2. Make a T-chart on a sheet of chart paper. Write two headings: *Fantasy* and *Real World*. Ask students to brainstorm the differences between fantasy and real world. Write students' responses under the correct category.
3. Explain to students that fantasy is a genre that uses magic and other supernatural forms as a primary element of *plot*, theme, and/or setting. As they read these types of stories, they will notice that the author may include clues or *foreshadowing* hints that will allow the reader to *predict* what will happen in the story. As you discuss fantasy writing with students, use the **Idea Completions** strategy (page 18) to introduce the vocabulary and develop students' oral language.

Procedure *(cont.)*

Some examples of idea completions include the following:

- The *plot* of a *story* is its…
- You may *predict* an event in a story by…
- An author may include *foreshadowing* hints or clues to make the readers…
- A *fantasy* story is not true, such as...

4. Distribute copies of *The Rock* reading passage (page 50) to students. Read the text aloud using expression to help set the tone for the surprising events in the story. Discuss with students some of the elements of a fantasy text. For example, students can be asked, "What examples of *foreshadowing* are present in this *story*?"
5. Review the **Vocabulary Journal** strategy (page 28) with students to remind them of the importance of having a place to routinely write about and reflect on vocabulary words that they are learning.
6. Distribute copies of the *Elements of a Fantasy Story* activity sheet (page 51) to students. Tell students that this activity is going to be a part of their vocabulary journals. Tell students they can use the words and concepts on their activity sheets to help them with their ideas.
7. Distribute copies of the *Fantasy Context Interpretation* assessment sheet (page 52) to students. Have students complete the assessment individually to see whether they understand how to correctly use the focus vocabulary words in context.

Differentiation

English language support—Discuss the fantasy story ideas with the students. Have them share their ideas orally and help them put their ideas into words to record on the activity sheet.

Below-level students—Continue to use the pictures from step 1. Record students' responses to help identify elements of fantasy.

Above-level students—Give students time to gather favorite fantasy stories and make a list of the common elements of the genre. Have them share the list with the rest of the class.

Name________________________________

The Rock

DIRECTIONS Read the passage.

Carson and Alex loved to walk in the woods behind Carson's house. It was freedom! They could explore, run, jump, hide—and still be able to hear Carson's mom if she called for them. These two best friends were happier playing together outside than doing anything else.

It was a cold autumn day when the two boys decided to run around and explore. The leaves were starting to change, and there was color everywhere. That is why it was so surprising that they did not just miss it: the rock. A bright-red, shiny, smooth rock. It sparkled in a way that was unusual for a rock, as if it were on fire inside. But there the rock was, underneath the tall, old pine tree that was always the home base for their baseball games. It was just sitting there, and then it caught the attention of both boys.

Carson saw the rock first, but Alex quickly noticed it and bent down to pick it up. Before either boy could say a word, they were suddenly transported to a new place altogether. It happened in the blink of an eye.

"Where are we?" Alex stammered.

"I have no idea," said Carson.

The two boys looked around. They were still in the woods, but things were different. It was no longer fall, for one thing. It was nighttime, and snow was on the ground.

"Where's my house?" Carson yelled.

The boys quickly realized that Carson's house was no longer there. In its place stood a small, one-room log cabin. Alex looked down. The rock was still in his hand. It was glowing a deep shade of purple now. Alex felt scared.

"Carson, what is this thing?" he asked.

"I don't know. Let me see it." Carson grabbed the rock, and then it happened. It was just as fast as before. They were going somewhere else.

Name_______________________________

Elements of a Fantasy Story

DIRECTIONS Look at the words in the Word Box. What have you learned about the parts of a fantasy story? Write about it using the new words from the Word Box.

Word Box	
fantasy	plot
foreshadow	predict

Name________________________________

Fantasy Context Interpretation

DIRECTIONS Read each sentence below. Then read the question and write your answer.

1. **Context:** The author *foreshadowed* that the main character was going to be in big trouble.

   Question: How does the reader feel about this?

   Answer: ____

   ____

2. **Context:** The mother could *predict* that the toddler was going to throw a tantrum.

   Question: What does the mother think about that?

   Answer: ____

   ____

3. **Context:** The *plot* of the story was full of suspense.

   Question: What does the reader think about this?

   Answer: ____

   ____

4. **Context:** The students were eager to learn about *fantasy* writing.

   Question: How do the students feel about this?

   Answer: ____

   ____

Let's Talk Fiction

Featured Academic Vocabulary Strategies

- **Questions, Reasons, and Examples:** Developing Oral Language (page 12)
- **Vocabulary Diagram:** Teaching Words (page 24)

Standards

- **McREL:** Students will read a variety of literary passages and texts.
- **McREL:** Students will understand level-appropriate sight words and vocabulary.
- **TESOL:** Students will use appropriate learning strategies to construct and apply academic knowledge.

Materials

- *Opening Day* (page 55)
- *Vocabulary Diagram: Fiction* (page 56)
- *Show You Know About Fiction* (page 57)

Focus Vocabulary Words	
Specialized Content Vocabulary	**General Academic Vocabulary**
fiction mood nonfiction tone	identify

Procedure

1. Begin the lesson by asking students to distinguish between *fiction* and *nonfiction*. Ask students to brainstorm words, ideas, concepts, and examples of how these two genres are different and similar.

2. Distribute copies of the *Opening Day* reading passage (page 55) to students. Read the text aloud to students. As you read the passage, discuss the vocabulary words. Use the story to help teach these concepts. For example, you may say *The tone in the author's writing expressed eagerness for the main character to make a goal.*

3. Use the **Questions, Reasons, and Examples** strategy (page 12) to further discuss the focus vocabulary words and help students share information and examples related to these new concepts. Pose questions to students that they have to answer by using the vocabulary words in a relevant and appropriate way. Some examples include the following:

   - What are some examples in the reading passage that help you *identify the mood in the story?*
   - What is a book you enjoy that has a specific *tone*?
   - Would you rather read a *fiction* or *nonfiction* book? Why?

Procedure *(cont.)*

4. Review the **Vocabulary Diagram** strategy (page 24) with students. Explain to students that they will analyze the word *fiction*. Distribute copies of the *Vocabulary Diagram: Fiction* activity sheet (page 56) to students. Tell students that this activity will be a method for them to learn even more about the word *fiction*.
5. Have students work independently or in pairs to complete the vocabulary diagram. Then have student volunteers share their work with the class.
6. Distribute copies of the *Show You Know About Fiction* assessment sheet (page 57) to students. Have students complete the assessment individually to determine whether they understand how to correctly use the focus vocabulary words in context.

Differentiation

English language support—Use relevant examples from students' own lives to help explain some of the vocabulary, such as *mood*, *tone*, *notice*, and *opinion*.

Below-level students—Complete the Vocabulary Diagram as a small group. Guide students as they fill out the activity sheet.

Above-level students—Have students write short pieces of fiction, and then explain how their examples are related to the new focus vocabulary words.

Name________________________________

Opening Day

DIRECTIONS Read the passage. Then answer the questions below.

It was the first day of the season. Madison was about to play her first soccer game, and she was nervous. Madison got into position in the goal and tried to stay focused on the ball. It was now heading straight for her.

One player was heading straight for the goal. She took a shot, and the ball sailed right into the goal's net.

Madison was crushed. She wanted to cry. During halftime, the coach gave a pep talk. "You girls are looking great. Hang in there!" he said. 'Maybe I can do this,' she thought. She ran back to her position.

Here they came again, headed for the goal. Someone kicked the ball hard—right into Madison's hands! A great save! The crowd erupted into cheers. Madison was thrilled.

Madison's team lost, but she did not care. It was going to be a great season, because Madison knew they would make it to the playoffs in Jupiter.

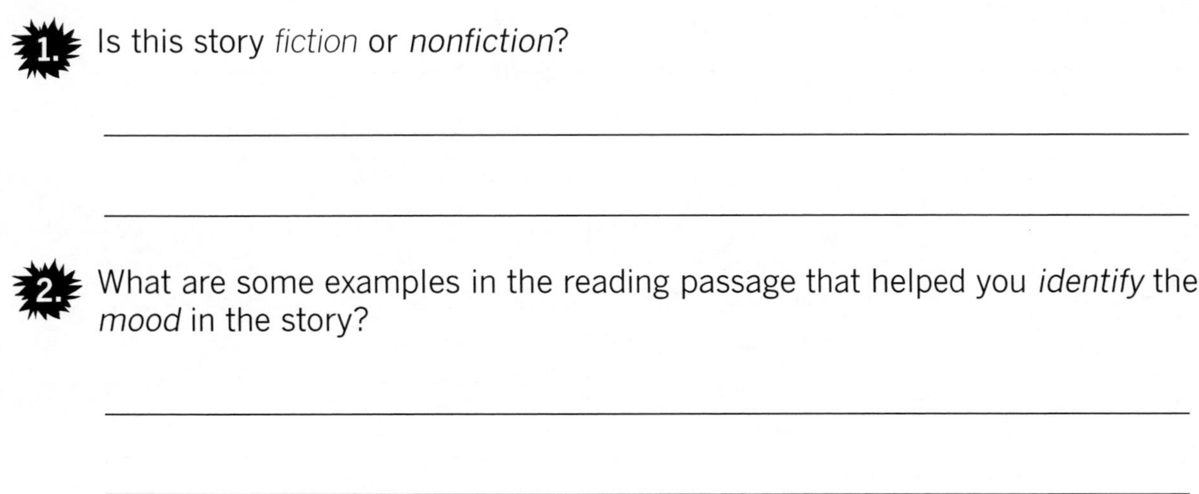

1. Is this story *fiction* or *nonfiction*?

____

____

2. What are some examples in the reading passage that helped you *identify* the *mood* in the story?

____

____

Name________________________________

Vocabulary Diagram: Fiction

DIRECTIONS Record your responses for the word *fiction*. Write your answers below.

Word:	**Synonyms:** **Antonyms:**
Other Forms of the Word:	**Example:**
Picture:	**Sentence:** ______________________ ______________________ ______________________ ______________________ ______________________ ______________________

Name________________________________

Show You Know About Fiction

DIRECTIONS Read each pair of vocabulary words. Then write a sentence that uses the words appropriately in context.

1. **Vocabulary words:** *identify, mood*

   Student response: ____

   ____

   ____

2. **Vocabulary words:** *identify, tone*

   Student response: ____

   ____

   ____

3. **Vocabulary words:** *fiction, nonfiction*

   Student response: ____

   ____

   ____

4. **Vocabulary words:** *fiction, tone*

   Student response: ____

   ____

5. **Vocabulary words:** *mood, nonfiction*

   Student response: ____

   ____

   ____

A Lesson in a Fable

Featured Academic Vocabulary Strategies

- **Cloze Sentences:** Developing Oral Language (page 14)
- **Vocabulary Journal:** Independent Word Learning (page 28)

Standards

- **McREL:** Students will read a variety of literary passages and texts.
- **McREL:** Students will understand level-appropriate sight words and vocabulary.
- **TESOL:** Students will use appropriate learning strategies to construct and apply academic knowledge.

Materials

- chart paper
- marker
- *The Lion and the Mouse* (page 60)
- *Reflections on Fables* (page 61)
- *Fable Word Translations* (page 62)

Focus Vocabulary Words	
Specialized Content Vocabulary	**General Academic Vocabulary**
fable moral story tradition	conflict

Procedure

1. Begin the lesson by reviewing with students what they know about *fables*. As a group, determine the elements of a fable. Write students' responses on a sheet of chart paper. Guide students to the idea that a fable usually is a short *story*, has animal characters with human qualities, and has a *moral* or lesson at the end of the story.

2. Introduce the vocabulary words *conflict*, *moral*, and *tradition*. Discuss how the vocabulary words are relevant to fables. Use the **Cloze Sentences** strategy (page 14) to reinforce students' knowledge of the new vocabulary and to give them the opportunity to share their ideas orally. Some examples of cloze sentences may include the following:
   - The ________ of a ________ is often the event that changes the course of the plot. (*conflict; story*)
   - A short story with a moral or lesson at the end is called a ________. (*fable*)
   - A ________ of a fable is also known as a lesson. (*moral*)
   - A long-established custom or belief is known as a ________. (*tradition*)

Procedure *(cont.)*

3. Distribute copies of the *The Lion and the Mouse* reading passage (page 60) to students. Read the text aloud to students. Then have them read the fable in pairs. Have them discuss in pairs about what elements of a fable they are able to identify. Ask students to share information about the animal characters, the human qualities, and the moral at the end of the fable.

4. Use the **Vocabulary Journal** strategy (page 28) with students to remind them of the importance of having a place to routinely write about and reflect on vocabulary words that they are learning.

5. Distribute copies of the *Reflections on Fables* activity sheet (page 61) to students. Tell students that these activity sheets are going to be a part of their vocabulary journal. Tell students that on the activity sheet they will be recording ideas they have after listening to *The Lion and the Mouse*.

6. Distribute copies of the *Fable Word Translations* assessment sheet (page 62) to students. Have students complete the assessment individually to see whether they understand how to correctly use the focus vocabulary words.

Differentiation

English language support—Allow students to act out *The Lion and the Mouse* fable in pairs to better understand the story and the genre of fables.

Below-level students—Read several different fables to students over the course of several days if possible, so that they can begin to understand the tone and style of a fable. Use these fables to help solidify understanding of the focus vocabulary words.

Above-level students—Have students take what they have learned from the new vocabulary and ask them to write their own fables. Remind them to include the essential elements of a fable in their own writing.

Name________________________________

The Lion and the Mouse

DIRECTIONS Read the passage. Then answer the questions below.

Once when a lion was asleep, a little mouse began running up and down upon him. This soon wakened the lion, who placed his huge paw upon him and opened his big jaw to swallow him.

"Pardon, King. Forgive me this time, I shall never forget it. Who knows—I may be able to do you a favor one of these days," cried the little mouse.

The lion was so tickled at the idea of the mouse being able to help him that he lifted his paw and let him go.

Some time after, the lion was caught in a trap, and the hunters, who desired to carry him alive to the king, tied him to a tree while they went in search of a wagon to carry him on.

Just then, the little mouse happened to pass by, and seeing the lion's sad plight, went up to him and soon gnawed away the ropes that bound the King.

"Was I not right?" said the little mouse.

Moral of the story: Little friends may prove great friends.

1. What were the *conflicts* in the story?

____

____

2. Why is this passage considered a *fable*?

____

____

Name________________________________

Reflections on Fables

DIRECTIONS Look at the words in the Word Box. What thoughts did you have about the fable you read? Use the words in the Word Box to share your ideas.

Word Box	
conflict	moral
culture	tradition
fable	

Name________________________________

Fable Word Translations

Read each original sentence below. Then translate each sentence from academic language into casual language. Be sure to show your understanding of the vocabulary words.

1. **Original sentence:** A *fable* is a *story* that is passed down within a culture from older generations.

   Student sentence: ____

   ____

2. **Original sentence:** The *moral* of a fable typically comes at the end of the *story*.

   Student sentence: ____

   ____

3. **Original sentence:** *Fables* are an important part of a written *tradition* within a culture.

   Student sentence: ____

   ____

4. **Original sentence:** A *conflict* can be an important part of any *story*.

   Student sentence: ____

   ____

5. **Original sentence:** A *moral* of a *fable* is slightly different than a theme of a *story*.

   Student sentence: ____

   ____

Writing Personal Narratives

Featured Academic Vocabulary Strategies

- **Have You Ever?:** Developing Oral Language (page 10)
- **Vocabulary Diagram:** Teaching Words (page 24)

Standards

- **McREL:** Students will write narrative accounts, such as poems and stories.
- **McREL:** Students will use level-appropriate vocabulary in speech.
- **TESOL:** Students will use appropriate learning strategies to construct and apply academic knowledge.

Materials

- *A Personal Narrative* (page 65)
- *Vocabulary Diagram: Narrative* (page 66)
- *Personal Narrative Context Interpretation* (page 67)

Focus Vocabulary Words	
Specialized Content Vocabulary	**General Academic Vocabulary**
chronological main idea narrative perspective	conflict

Procedure

1. Review what a personal *narrative* is and how to identify this type of writing. Tell students that a personal narrative is nonfiction writing about the author's own life and experiences. It is written in *chronological* order and also written from the author's *perspective*.
2. Share an example of a personal narrative with the class (e.g., experience of becoming a teacher). As the story is shared integrate the components of the story such as the *main idea* (wanting to become a teacher), *conflict* (finding it difficult to find a job), and resolution (being persistent in finding a job).
3. Use the **Have You Ever?** strategy (page 10) to connect students' knowledge of the vocabulary words to their own personal experiences. The following examples can be used in the discussion:
   - When might you tell a story in *chronological* order?
   - What is a *conflict* you have had and how did you resolve it?
   - What type of personal *narrative* would you write about?
   - Reflect on a time when you had a different *perspective* than your friend.

Procedure *(cont.)*

4. Distribute copies of the *A Personal Narrative* activity sheet (page 65) to students. Tell students that they are going to practice writing their own personal narratives. Review the concepts and vocabulary words related to this genre of writing. If needed, share some important signal words such as *first*, *next*, and *after* that can be included in their narratives to signal the order of events. Provide students time to write their personal narrative texts. When they are finished, discuss the importance of reflecting on their work.

5. Use the **Vocabulary Diagram** strategy (page 24) with students. Explain that they will be analyzing the word *narrative*. Distribute copies of the *Vocabulary Diagram: Narrative* activity sheet (page 66) to students. Tell students that this activity will be a method for them to learn even more about a personal narrative. Have students complete the vocabulary diagram. Then have student volunteers share their work with the class.

6. Distribute copies of the *Personal Narrative Context Interpretation* assessment sheet (page 67) to students. Have students complete the assessment individually to see whether they understand how to correctly apply their knowledge of new vocabulary to their own personal experiences.

Differentiation

English language support—Work as a group to draft a personal narrative. Use a familiar shared experience in your classroom (e.g., field trip, assembly, special holiday) as a topic.

Below-level students—Provide students with sentence frames to help them write their personal narrative texts.

Above-level students—Have students work independently to complete their Vocabulary Diagram activity sheets, using more challenging vocabulary.

Name________________________________

A Personal Narrative

DIRECTIONS Write your own personal narrative in the space below.

Name________________________________

Vocabulary Diagram: Narrative

DIRECTIONS Record your responses for the word *narrative*. Write your answers below.

Word:	**Synonyms:** **Antonyms:**
Other Forms of the Word:	**Example:**
Picture:	**Sentence:** ____________________ ____________________ ____________________ ____________________ ____________________ ____________________

Name________________________________

Personal Narrative Context Interpretation

DIRECTIONS Read each sentence below. Then read the question and write your answer.

1. **Context:** The speaker read a personal *narrative* that involved him in the *story*.

   Question: How might the speaker feel about this?

   Answer: ____

   ____

2. **Context:** The two friends had a *conflict* over a toy.

   Question: What do the friends think about the conflict?

   Answer: ____

   ____

3. **Context:** The students did not understand the *main idea* of the story.

   Question: What do the students think about this?

   Answer: ____

   ____

4. **Context:** The little girl was eager to read about the author's *perspective* on the story.

   Question: How does the little girl feel about this?

   Answer: ____

   ____

Vivid and Colorful Descriptive Writing

Featured Academic Vocabulary Strategies

- **Idea Completions**: Developing Oral Language (page 18)
- **Ten Important Words:** Developing Word Consciousness (page 20)

Standards

- **McREL:** Students will use descriptive and precise language that clarifies and enhances ideas.
- **McREL:** Students will use strategies to write for a variety of purposes.
- **TESOL:** Students will use English to obtain, process, construct, and provide subject-matter information in spoken and written form.

Materials

- *How to Write with Descriptive Language* (page 70)
- *Descriptive Writing Practice* (page 71)
- chart paper
- marker
- sticky notes
- *Show You Know About Descriptive Writing* (page 72)

Focus Vocabulary Words	
Specialized Content Vocabulary	**General Academic Vocabulary**
figurative language figure of speech	description detail visualize

Procedure

1. Before beginning this lesson, use the **Idea Completions** strategy (page 18) and create sentences for each of the vocabulary words. Make sure to include clue words within the sentence that will help students guess the correct vocabulary words and learn more about their definitions. The following are some examples of Idea Completions:
   - Sometimes authors include a lot of *detail* in their writing so that you can *visualize*…
   - A written or verbal *description* may tell…
   - Instead of using literal words, *figurative language* is…
2. Write the following sentence on the board: *I felt hunger before lunchtime.* Discuss what this sentence means and how it sounds. Lead students to the idea that the sentence is simple and boring. Encourage students to add more *detail* or a *figure of speech* (e.g., I could eat a horse!) to help make the sentence more vivid.
3. Introduce your Idea Completions sentences. Discuss the sentences as a class, and write students' responses on the board.

Procedure *(cont.)*

4. Use the **Ten Important Words** strategy (page 20) with students. Tell students that they will be looking through a reading passage for ten words they think are important about the topic of descriptive writing. Distribute copies of the *How to Write with Descriptive Language* activity sheet (page 70) to students. Tell students to read the passage and circle ten words they think are important. When students are finished, provide them time to share their findings with a partner and to write their words on sticky notes to analyze students' findings as a class..

5. Distribute copies of the *Descriptive Writing Practice* activity sheet (page 71) to students. Read the paragraph aloud. Tell students that they are going to rewrite the paragraph using more descriptive, vivid, sensory language. Encourage students to use figurative language. When students are finished with their work, ask them to share their writing in pairs.

6. Distribute copies of the *Show You Know About Descriptive Writing* assessment sheet (page 72) to students. Have students complete the assessment individually to determine whether they understand how to correctly use the vocabulary words.

Differentiation

English language support—Complete the *Writing Practice* activity sheet as a small group. Make suggestions for how students can incorporate more vivid and descriptive language.

Below-level students—Help students complete the **Ten Important Words** strategy by reading the text aloud to them and helping them identify the important words.

Above-level students—Have students sort their words into various categories. Ask students to share their ideas with the rest of the group.

Name________________________________

How to Write with Descriptive Language

Read the passage below. Find ten words you think are important about how to write with descriptive language. Circle your words in the reading passage and then write them in the boxes below.

Descriptive language makes the words on the page come alive in the minds of the readers. It helps readers to visualize the events in the text.

Figurative language is one way to incorporate descriptive language into your writing. This means using words to exaggerate or slightly change the literal meaning of a word or sentence. A figure of speech is a type of figurative language. Metaphors and similes are figures of speech that an author may use to compare two different things in a story. Personification, hyperbole, and irony are all other examples of figurative language. These techniques make your writing more interesting and colorful by using language in a way that clearly explains things to the reader.

Relying on the five senses is a good idea, too. If you share how or what a character sees, hears, smells, touches, and feels, then your reader will better understand the story.

Important Words:	

Name________________________________

Descriptive Writing Practice

DIRECTIONS Read the paragraph below. Rewrite the story using more descriptive language.

It was a hot day. The cat was walking down the road. The cat saw a mouse. He ran to try to catch the mouse. He climbed a fence. Then he fell into a pond. The mouse got away. The cat hated to be wet. But the cold water felt good. The cat got out of the water and kept walking. He went home. He took a nap.

Name________________________________

Show You Know About Descriptive Writing

DIRECTIONS Read each pair of vocabulary words. Then write a sentence that uses the words appropriately in context.

1. **Vocabulary Words:** *visualize, figurative language*

   Student response: ____

   ____

   ____

2. **Vocabulary Words:** *visualize, detail*

   Student response: ____

   ____

   ____

3. **Vocabulary Words:** *description, figure of speech*

   Student response: ____

   ____

   ____

4. **Vocabulary Words:** *figurative language, detail*

   Student response: ____

   ____

   ____

5. **Vocabulary Words:** *detail, figure of speech*

   Student response: ____

   ____

   ____

Sending a Letter

Featured Academic Vocabulary Strategies

- **Cloze Sentences:** Developing Oral Language (page 14)
- **Vocabulary Journal:** Independent Word Learning (page 28)

Standards

- **McREL:** Students will write personal letters.
- **McREL:** Students will use level-appropriate vocabulary in speech.
- **TESOL:** Students will use appropriate learning strategies to construct and apply academic knowledge.

Materials

- *Completing Sentences* (page 75)
- *Your Friendly Letter* (page 76)
- *Letter Word Translations* (page 77)

Focus Vocabulary Words	
Specialized Content Vocabulary	**General Academic Vocabulary**
body closing date greeting signature	organize

Procedure

1. Tell students that they are going to learn how to write a friendly letter. Begin the lesson by asking students what is included in a letter. As students brainstorm ideas, guide students to include the main parts of a letter: the *date*, a *greeting*, the *body*, a *closing*, and a *signature*. If applicable, show students a sample of a letter including the main parts that are discussed.

2. Discuss briefly with students the steps that they may take to write a friendly letter. Discuss with students why a writer would need to *organize* his or her ideas within the letter.

3. Use the **Cloze Sentences** strategy (page 14) to reinforce students' knowledge of the new vocabulary. Some examples of cloze sentences include the following:

   - The ________ of the letter is the main part. *(body)*
   - You might write *Sincerely* or *Yours truly* for a ________. *(closing)*
   - The ________ on a letter tells when it was written. *(date)*
   - Adding your name is called the ________. *(signature)*

Procedure *(cont.)*

4. Use the **Vocabulary Journal** strategy (page 28) with students to remind them of the importance of having a place to routinely write about the vocabulary words that they are learning.
5. Distribute copies of the *Completing Sentences* activity sheet (page 75) to students. Tell students that this activity sheet is going to be a part of their vocabulary journal. Tell students that on the activity sheet they will be reviewing and practicing writing sentences using the vocabulary words they just learned.
6. Distribute copies of *Your Friendly Letter* activity sheet (page 76) to students. Tell students that they will be writing their own friendly letters in the space provided. Remind students to incorporate the main parts of a letter.
7. Distribute copies of the *Letter Word Translations* assessment sheet (page 77) to students. Have students complete the assessment individually to determine whether they understand how to correctly use the focus vocabulary words in context.

Differentiation

English language support—Work with students in guiding them to draft their friendly letters. If possible, show them sample letters as a visual.

Below-level students—Provide students with sentence frames to help them write friendly letters independently.

Above-level students—Talk with students about the difference between writing a friendly letter and a more formal business letter. Ask students to write formal letters that are relevant to a current unit of study. They may want to write to a museum, a newspaper, or your local government.

Name________________________________

Completing Sentences

DIRECTIONS Complete the first three sentences below using words from the Word Box.

Word Box	
body	greeting
closing	organize
date	signature

1. The ________________ of the letter may be divided into paragraphs.
2. Writing your name at the bottom of the letter means including your ____________________ .
3. All writers should __________________ their work when they are finished to make sure that no further changes are needed.

Now write three of your own sentences with the remaining vocabulary words. Trade your paper with a classmate and have him or her complete the sentences.

4. ____

____

5. ____

____

6. ____

____

Name________________________________

Your Friendly Letter

DIRECTIONS Write your own friendly letter in the space below. Make sure to include all parts of the letter.

Name________________________________

Letter Word Translations

Read each original sentence below. Then translate each sentence from academic language into casual language.

1. **Original sentence:** After I write my letter, I will add my *signature.*

   Student sentence: ________________________________

   ____

2. **Original sentence:** The *body* of a letter comes after the *greeting.*

   Student sentence: ________________________________

   ____

3. **Original sentence:** Why do authors include the *date* on a letter?

   Student sentence: ________________________________

   ____

4. **Original sentence:** If I am writing to someone I know well, I can use a casual *closing.*

   Student sentence: ________________________________

   ____

5. **Original sentence:** Please make sure to *organize* your ideas before you write a *letter.*

   Student sentence: ________________________________

   ____

Expository Texts

Featured Academic Vocabulary Strategies

- **Alike and Different:** Developing Oral Language (page 16)
- **Content Links:** Teaching Words (page 26)

Standards

- **McREL:** Students will write expository compositions.
- **McREL:** Students will use strategies to write for a variety of purposes.
- **TESOL:** Students will use English to obtain, process, construct, and provide subject-matter information in spoken and written form.

Materials

- *Writing Plan* (page 80)
- index cards
- *Making Content Links* (page 81)
- *Personal Examples About Expository Texts* (page 82)

Focus Vocabulary Words	
Specialized Content Vocabulary	**General Academic Vocabulary**
expository	clarify define explain inform instruct

Procedure

1. Begin the lesson by reviewing with students what they already know about *expository* texts. Make sure that students understand that expository writing is nonfiction writing. An author of expository writing is hoping to *inform*, *explain*, *clarify*, *define*, or *instruct* the reader.
2. Share the general academic vocabulary words with students, giving an explanation and example for each word. Use the **Alike and Different** strategy (page 16) to help students make connections among the words.
3. Write the selected vocabulary pairs on the board. Ask students to think about what they know about each of these words. Then ask students to discuss how the words are similar and different. Repeat this process for other word pairs from the vocabulary list.

Procedure *(cont.)*

4. Tell students that they are going to use what they have learned about the vocabulary words to plan and write their own expository texts. Distribute copies of the *Writing Plan* activity sheet (page 80) to students and explain that they will be using this graphic organizer to plan for an expository writing assignment. Give students time to plan their expository texts and ask them to share their ideas in pairs. Encourage students to brainstorm additional words they learned that are related to this type of writing. End the list when there is one word for every student in the class.
5. Record the words on index cards and distribute one card to each student. Complete the **Content Links** strategy (page 26) with students to solidify their comprehension of the words necessary to understand the content of this lesson.
6. Distribute copies of the *Making Content Links* activity sheet (page 81) to students. With the partner with whom they linked, have students complete the activity sheet explaining how their words are related.
7. Distribute copies of the *Personal Examples About Expository Texts* assessment sheet (page 82) to students. Have students complete the assessment individually to determine whether they understand how to correctly apply their knowledge of new vocabulary to their own personal experiences.

Differentiation

English language support—Allow students to create simple sentences of their ideas. Help students expand on their ideas if writing expository texts in the future.

Below-level students—Complete the writing assignment as a small group. Help guide students as you model how to write an expository text.

Above-level students—Have students find various examples of expository texts. Encourage them to share their findings with their classmates.

Name________________________________

Writing Plan

DIRECTIONS Use the space below to plan your writing.

My Topic:

____

How I Will Organize My Ideas:

____

____

My Central Idea:

____

____

Supporting Idea #1:

____

____

____

Supporting Idea #2:

____

____

____

Supporting Idea #3:

____

____

____

Supporting Idea #4:

____

____

____

Name________________________________

Making Content Links

DIRECTIONS Write the words that you linked together in the spaces below and illustrate why they can be linked. Then write a short description of how and why the words are linked.

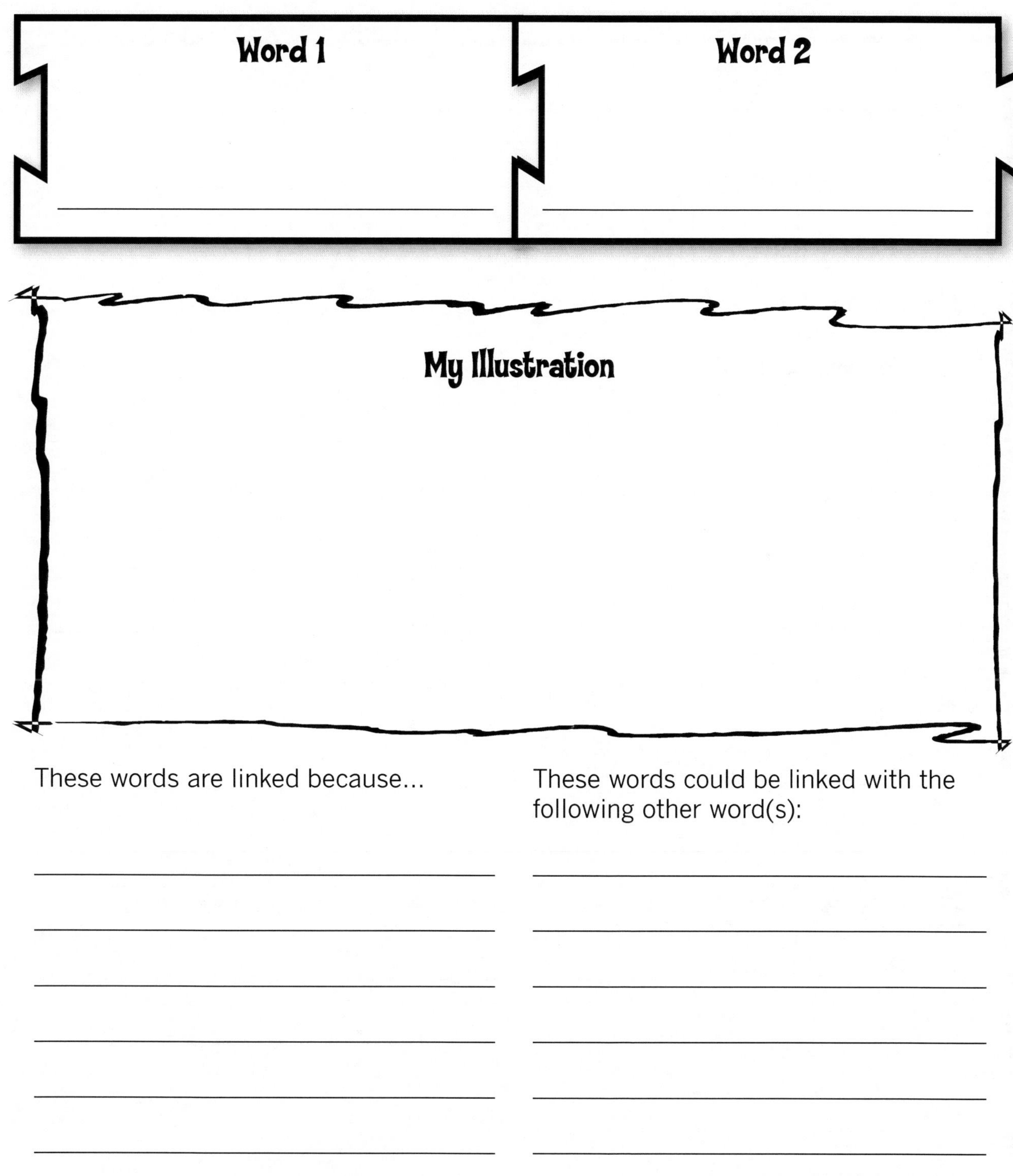

These words are linked because...

____

____

____

____

____

____

____

These words could be linked with the following other word(s):

____

____

____

____

____

____

____

Name________________________________

Personal Examples About Expository Texts

DIRECTIONS Read each prompt below. Then write a personal example for your response.

1. **Prompt:** When might you need to *explain* something at school?

   Personal Example:____

   ____

2. **Prompt:** Write about a time you *clarified* something to someone.

   Personal Example:____

   ____

3. **Prompt:** Tell of a time when you wrote using *expository* writing.

   Personal Example:____

   ____

4. **Prompt:** What type of text or story that you have read is often written to *inform*?

   Personal Example:____

   ____

5. **Prompt:** Write about a time you *instructed* someone to do something.

   Personal Example:____

   ____

Understanding and Creating Poetry

Focus Vocabulary Words	
Specialized Content Vocabulary	**General Academic Vocabulary**
descriptive phrase poetry simile	writing

Procedure

1. Explain to students that they are going to be discussing and writing *poetry*. Tell students that poetry has different styles of language and linguistic tools to describe ideas.
2. Discuss with students that poetry can be *descriptive* and discuss how descriptive language is helpful for the reader. Tell students that a form of descriptive writing can include using a *simile*. Explain that a simile uses the words *as* or *like* when describing two objects. Provide students with examples of similes.
3. Use the **Questions, Reasons, and Examples** strategy (page 12) to further discuss these vocabulary words and help students share information and examples related to these new concepts. Some examples include the following:
    - When might you use *descriptive* language to write a poem?
    - What *similes* have you heard recently?
    - In what situations might you write a *phrase* instead of a complete sentence?
    - When might you use *poetry* as a form of *writing*?

Featured Academic Vocabulary Strategies

- **Questions, Reasons, and Examples**: Developing Oral Language (page 12)
- **Word Hunt:** Developing Word Consciousness (page 22)

Standards

- **McREL:** Students will define characteristics and structural elements of a variety of literary genres.
- **McREL:** Students will use level-appropriate vocabulary in speech.
- **TESOL:** Students will use appropriate learning strategies to construct and apply academic knowledge.

Materials

- *Similes Galore!* (page 85)
- *Poetry Sample* (page 86)
- *Poetry Context Completion* (page 87)

Procedure *(cont.)*

4. Use the **Vocabulary Journal** strategy (page 28) with students to remind them of the importance of having a place to routinely write about vocabulary words that they are learning.

5. Distribute copies of the *Similes Galore!* activity sheet (page 85) to students. Tell students that this activity sheet is going to be a part of their vocabulary journal. Tell students that on the activity sheet they will be reviewing and practicing writing poems using similes. Allow students time to complete the activity sheet. When students are finished, have them share their sentences with the class.

6. Distribute copies of the *Poetry Sample* activity sheet (page 86) to students. Tell students that they will be writing poems. Challenge students to include examples of figurative language that has been discussed in this lesson. Encourage students to share their poetry.

8. Distribute copies of the *Poetry Context Completion* assessment sheet (page 87) to students. Have students complete the assessment individually to determine whether they understand how to correctly use the focus vocabulary words.

Differentiation

English language support—Create additional examples of similes for students. Then integrate sentence frames so students can practice writing their own poetry with the help of the frames.

Below-level students—Before having students write poetry independently, compose a poem as a group. Ask students to each contribute a line or word to your group poem.

Above-level students—Have students research additional figurative language. Have students share their findings with the class.

Name________________________________

Similes Galore!

Complete the poems by completing the simile and writing your answer in each line below. Remember, a simile describes two objects and uses the words *as* or *like*.

Lunchtime

The bell rings at noon.

Oh, no! I forgot my spoon.

It's shiny and silver
like ______________________.

Let's Play

I went outside to play.

The weather was ______________
like hairspray!

I ran inside and quickly hid.

It's no fun being a kid.

Backpack

My backpack is as heavy
as ______________________.

It's a feeling that everyone hates.

My back is as sore
as ______________________.

I'm ready to hit the floor!

Lost Glasses

Have you seen my glasses?

They're as red
as ______________________.

If I can't find them,

My dad will be steaming
like ______________________.

Name________________________________

Poetry Sample

DIRECTIONS Write your own poem in the space below. Try to include descriptive language using the methods that you have learned.

Name________________________________

Poetry Context Completion

DIRECTIONS Read each Context Completion sentence starter. Fill in the blank with information that correctly completes the sentence.

1. **Sentence starter:** Using a *simile* in poetry helps a reader to imagine by ____

____

____

2. **Sentence starter:** A *simile* makes a comparison by ________________

____

____

3. **Sentence starter:** To understand the meaning of a poem that includes *descriptive* writing, you have to ________________________

____

____

4. **Sentence starter:** The use of *descriptive* language in poetry is very important for the reader because ________________________

____

____

Patterns of Multiplication

Featured Academic Vocabulary Strategies

- **Idea Completions:** Developing Oral Language (page 18)
- **Content Links:** Teaching Words (page 26)

Standards

- **McREL:** Students will understand the properties of and the relationships among addition, subtraction, multiplication, and division.
- **McREL:** Students will respond to questions and comments.
- **TESOL:** Students will use appropriate learning strategies to construct and apply academic knowledge.

Materials

- *Multiplication Problems* (page 90)
- chart paper
- marker
- index cards
- *Making Connections* (page 91)
- *Show You Know About Multiplication* (page 92)

Focus Vocabulary Words	
Specialized Content Vocabulary	**General Academic Vocabulary**
multiply operation symbol	explain relationship

Procedure

1. Begin the lesson by reviewing with students that multiplication is repeated addition. Start with small numbers, such as $2 + 2 + 2$. Show students how that type of repeated addition is the same as 2×3. Ask students to share examples of how multiplication and addition are related.

2. As you continue to introduce these concepts to students, use the **Idea Completions** strategy (page 18) to introduce the vocabulary strategy and develop students' oral language. Some examples of idea completions include the following:

    - One way to *explain* your mathematical thinking is to…
    - Addition and multiplication have a *relationship* in that…
    - A multiplication number sentence includes a *symbol* that means…
    - When you follow the process of a mathematical *operation*, you must...
    - To *multiply* a number means to...

Procedure *(cont.)*

3. Distribute copies of the *Multiplication Problems* activity sheet (page 90) to students. Tell students that they are going to show an example of how multiplication can be found in their own lives. Have them think about different scenarios in which multiplication or repeated addition might play a part. Students will each draw a picture, write a number sentence, and then explain the idea.

4. When students are finished with their activity sheets, have them share their pictures in pairs. Based on this information, help facilitate a whole-class discussion about words and concepts related to multiplication. Remind students of the vocabulary words from the lesson by writing them on a sheet of chart paper. Then have students brainstorm additional words they have learned as a result of the lesson. End the list when there is one word for every student in the class.

5. Record the words on index cards and distribute one card to each student. Complete the **Content Links** strategy (page 26) with students to solidify their comprehension of the words necessary to understand the content of this lesson.

6. Distribute copies of the *Making Connections* activity sheet (page 91) to students. With the partner with whom they linked, have students complete the activity sheet to explain why and how their words are related. Circulate around the room as students complete this activity to ask further questions and monitor their comprehension of the vocabulary.

7. Distribute copies of the *Show You Know About Multiplication* assessment sheet (page 92) to students. Have students complete the assessment individually to determine whether they understand how to correctly use written vocabulary appropriately and in context.

Differentiation

English language support—Suggest ideas to students for how to complete the *Multiplication Problems* activity sheet. Choose ideas that are reflective of students' experiences and background.

Below-level students—Distribute vocabulary for the Content Links strategy that is appropriate and familiar to students. Check for comprehension before they begin mingling and talking with others about their assigned words.

Above-level students—Have students work in pairs and write Idea Completions sentences for each other. Have them share their sentences with the class when they are finished.

Name________________________________

Multiplication Problems

DIRECTIONS Think about how multiplication or repeated addition is found in your own life. Draw a picture in the box below to show your idea. Then write a number sentence and explain your idea.

An Example of Multiplication in My Life:

Number Sentence:

Write about your idea.

____

____

____

____

____

Name________________________________

Making Connections

DIRECTIONS Write the words that you linked together in the spaces below and illustrate why they can be linked. Then write a short description of how and why the words are linked.

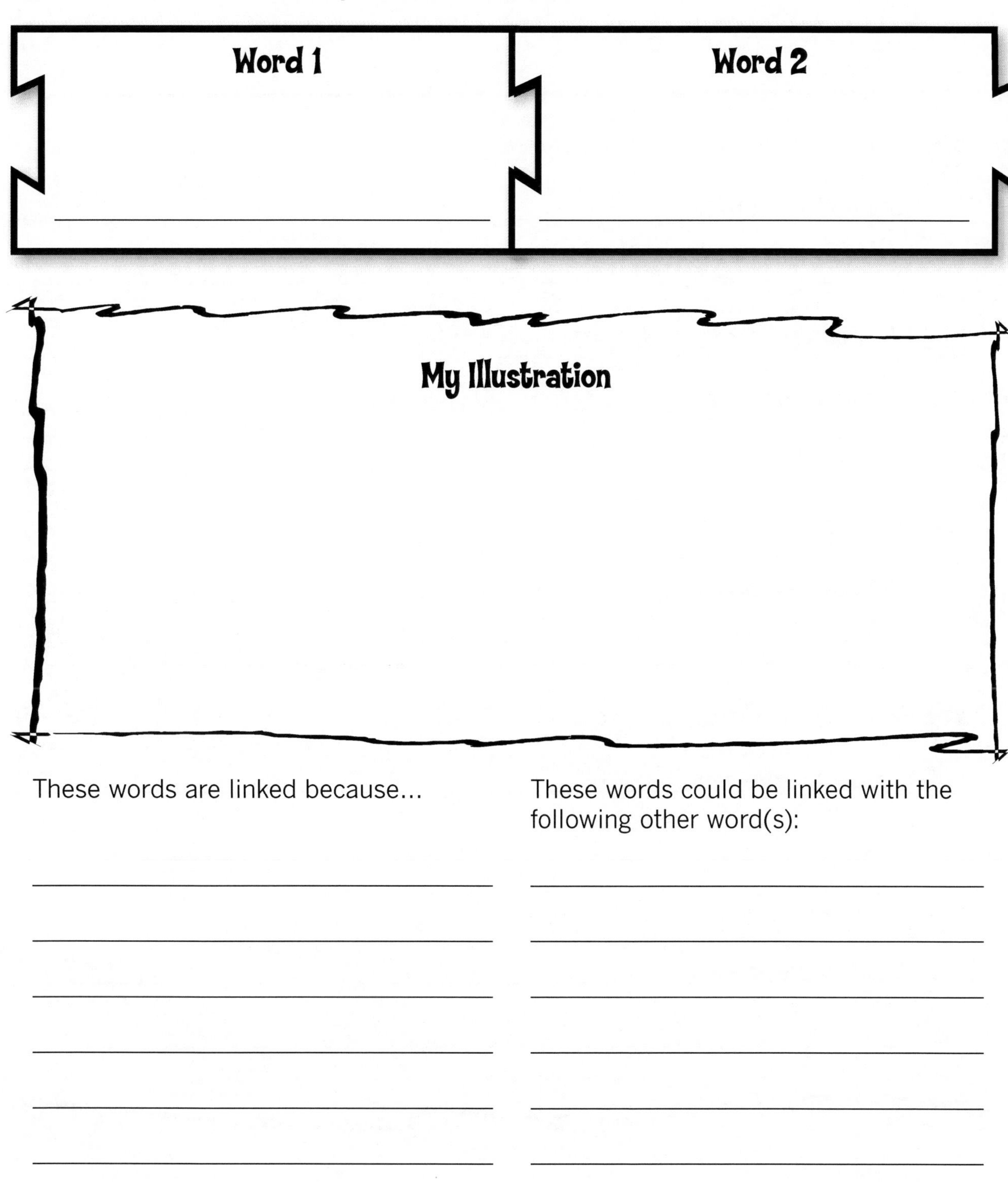

These words are linked because...

____

____

____

____

____

____

____

These words could be linked with the following other word(s):

____

____

____

____

____

____

____

Name________________________________

Show You Know About Multiplication

DIRECTIONS Read each pair of vocabulary words. Then write a sentence that uses the words appropriately in context.

1. **Vocabulary words:** *symbol, operation*

   Student response: ____

   ____

2. **Vocabulary words:** *multiply, symbol*

   Student response: ____

   ____

3. **Vocabulary words:** *relationship, operation*

   Student response: ____

   ____

4. **Vocabulary words:** *operation, multiply*

   Student response: ____

   ____

5. **Vocabulary words:** *explain, symbol*

   Student response: ____

   ____

Dividing It All Up

Featured Academic Vocabulary Strategies

- **Questions, Reasons, and Examples:** Developing Oral Language (page 12)
- **Vocabulary Journal:** Independent Word Learning (page 28)

Standards

- **McREL:** Students will multiply and divide whole numbers.
- **McREL:** Students will understand level-appropriate sight words and vocabulary.
- **TESOL:** Students will use appropriate learning strategies to construct and apply academic knowledge.

Materials

- chart paper
- marker
- *Dividing It All Up* (page 95)
- *Dividend, Divisor, and Quotient* (page 96)
- *Yes-No-Why?: Division* (page 97)
- sticky notes

Focus Vocabulary Words	
Specialized Content Vocabulary	**General Academic Vocabulary**
divide dividend divisor quotient	problem strategy

Procedure

1. Draw 12 cookies on a sheet of chart paper. Tell students that there are 12 cookies in the picture. Ask them to consider how they would *divide* the 12 cookies equally among 4 friends. Have students briefly talk in pairs to discuss their ideas about how to solve the *problem*.
2. Bring students back together as a group, and discuss the answer to your question as well as the strategy in which students figured out the answer. Have student volunteers share their ideas.
3. Use your example to write a number sentence for the word problem you shared (12 ÷ 4). Use the number sentence to introduce the vocabulary words *dividend*, *divisor*, and *quotient*.
4. As you introduce these concepts to students, use the **Questions, Reasons, and Examples** strategy (page 12) to further discuss these vocabulary words and help students share information and examples related to these new concepts. Ask questions that students have to answer by using the vocabulary in a relevant and appropriate way.

Procedure *(cont.)*

Some examples include the following:

- There are many ways to solve math problems. What *strategy* do you use to solve a division *problem*?
- Many things can be *divided*. When is a time that you had to *divide* something into parts?

5. Distribute copies of the *Dividing It All Up* activity sheet (page 95) to students. Tell students that they are going to write about and solve three separate division problems. When students are finished with their activity sheets, have them share their work and answers in pairs. Then review the work as a group.
6. Use the **Vocabulary Journal** strategy (page 28) with students to remind them of the importance of having a place to routinely write about vocabulary words that they are learning.
7. Distribute copies of the *Dividend, Divisor, and Quotient* activity sheet (page 96) to students. Tell students that this activity sheet is going to be a part of their vocabulary journal. Tell students that on the activity sheet they will be reviewing the vocabulary words they just learned. Allow students time to complete the worksheet and share their sentences with the class.
8. Distribute copies of the *Yes-No-Why?: Division* assessment sheet (page 97) to students. Have students complete the assessment individually to determine whether they understand how to correctly decide whether a word's real-world application is appropriate.

Differentiation

English language support—Help students discuss vocabulary words using the Questions, Reasons, and Examples strategy by providing sentence starters for students to use in their answers.

Below-level students—Allow students to use manipulatives to help them solve the division problems. Discuss the strategies that students used and help them communicate those strategies in writing.

Above-level students—Have students write a short explanation of the various strategies they use to solve division problems. Encourage them to use new vocabulary in their explanations, and then share them with the rest of the group.

Name________________________________

Dividing It All Up

DIRECTIONS Look at the division problems below. Fill in the blanks about each problem.

1. **15 ÷ 3**

The *dividend* is: ________________________________

The *divisor* is: ________________________________

Write an equation that shows the solution to the *problem.* ____________

Describe the *strategy* you used to solve the equation. ____________

____

2. **24 ÷ 6**

The *dividend* is: ________________________________

The *divisor* is: ________________________________

Write an equation that shows the solution to the *problem.* ____________

Describe the *strategy* you used to solve the equation. ____________

____

3. **18 ÷ 2**

The *dividend* is: ________________________________

The *divisor* is: ________________________________

Write an equation that shows the solution to the *problem.* ____________

Describe the *strategy* you used to solve the equation. ____________

____

Name________________________________

Dividend, Divisor, and Quotient

DIRECTIONS Look at the definitions of the words *dividend, divisor*, and *quotient* in the box below. Then look at the boxes with the division number sentences. Draw a picture in each box showing the number sentence listed. Make sure to label the parts of your number sentence.

dividend—the number being divided

divisor—the number that will divide the dividend exactly

quotient—result of a division

21 ÷ 3 = _____

20 ÷ 2 = _____

12 ÷ 6 = _____

Name________________________________

Yes-No-Why?: Division

Read each sentence below. Think about whether the context makes sense. Then write your response. Use the following sentence stems to begin your sentence:

- This makes sense because...
- This does not make sense because...
- This seems logical because...
- This seems illogical because...

1. **Sentence:** A division equation includes a *divisor* and a *dividend.*

   Response: ____

   ____

2. **Sentence:** The only way to solve a division word *problem* is to use a calculator.

   Response: ____

   ____

3. **Sentence:** A *strategy* to solve a division problem is to draw an illustration.

   Response: ____

   ____

4. **Sentence:** A *quotient* is the number you get from the division of one number by another.

   Response: ____

   ____

Making Sense of 3-D Shapes

Featured Academic Vocabulary Strategies

- **Alike and Different:** Developing Oral Language (page 16)
- **Clue Hunt:** Independent Word Learning (page 30)

Standards

- **McREL:** Students will know basic geometric language for describing and naming shapes.
- **McREL:** Students will use level-appropriate vocabulary in speech.
- **TESOL:** Students will use English to obtain, process, construct, and provide subject-matter information in spoken and written form.

Materials

- examples of 3-D shapes (optional)
- *Shape Attributes* (page 100)
- *Shapes in the Real World* (page 101)
- *Personal Examples of 3-D Shapes* (page 102)

Focus Vocabulary Words	
Specialized Content Vocabulary	**General Academic Vocabulary**
cube cylinder sphere	compare

Procedure

1. Begin the lesson by reviewing with students what they already know about 3-D shapes. Show the group a few different examples of 3-D shapes and discuss basic information about those shapes. For example, students can be shown a *cube* and told, "This is a *cube*. It is a 3-D shape with 6 faces and 12 edges."
2. Share the vocabulary words with students. Continue to use the 3-D shapes to discuss the terms and share the definitions of the vocabulary words.
3. Use the **Alike and Different** strategy (page 16) to help students make connections among words and focus on new vocabulary.

Procedure *(cont.)*

4. Write the vocabulary pair *cube* and *cylinder* on the board. Ask students to think about what they know about each of these words. Then ask students to discuss how the meanings of the words are similar and different. Encourage students to *compare* the shapes. Record student ideas on a Venn diagram on the board. Repeat this process for other word pairs from the vocabulary list.

5. Distribute copies of the *Shape Attributes* activity sheet (page 100) to students. Explain to students that they will be filling out the chart with information about each 3-D shape that is listed. Have students complete their activity sheets in pairs. Ask them to share their ideas as they work.

6. Use the **Clue Hunt** strategy (page 30) with students and discuss how context clues can be an essential tool for understanding new and unfamiliar vocabulary. Review with students what context clues are and explain that they will be doing a clue hunt for the vocabulary words they are learning.

7. Distribute copies of the *Shapes in the Real World* reading passage (page 101) to students. Read the passage aloud to students. Have students reread the passage and circle any vocabulary words and context clues they find within the passage.

8. Distribute copies of the *Personal Examples of 3-D Shapes* assessment sheet (page 102) to students. Have students complete the assessment individually to determine whether they understand how to correctly apply their knowledge of new vocabulary to their own personal experiences.

Differentiation

English language support—Bring in two related (but slightly different) objects and use them to help students better understand the concepts of *compare* and *describe*.

Below-level students—Read the text with students in a small group and check for understanding as you read together.

Above-level students—Have students scan mathematics-related materials to find examples of each of the four types of context clues to share with the group. Talk about each example and why it provides more information about unfamiliar vocabulary.

Name______________________________

Shape Attributes

DIRECTIONS Fill in the chart with the information you have learned about 3-D shapes.

Name of 3-D Shape	Number of Edges	Number of Faces	Real-World Example
cube			
cylinder			
sphere			

What are some similarities and differences between the 3-D shapes?

____

____

____

____

____

____

____

____

____

____

____

____

____

Name________________________________

Shapes in the Real World

DIRECTIONS Read the passage below. Circle the vocabulary words and context clues you find. Then fill out the table below with your findings.

If you look closely, you will see 3-D shapes all around you. You might even find them in unlikely places.

Look around your classroom. Any type of ball is an example of a sphere. A sphere does not have any edge or vertices, but it has one face. If you spot a box, you will notice that it is a solid figure with six equal-sized faces and 12 edges. This type of figure is called a cube. You or a classmate might have even brought a cylinder in your lunch if you have a can of some kind. A cylinder has two edges and three faces.

Outside of the classroom are even more examples of these 3-D shapes. Some shapes are congruent. Other shapes are dissimilar. When you compare, or evaluate, two shapes to discover similarities or differences, you will notice that all shapes have unique qualities. This is why looking for shapes can be so much fun!

Words	Context Clues in Text
sphere	
cube	
cylinder	

Name________________________________

Personal Examples of 3-D Shapes

DIRECTIONS Read each prompt. Then write a personal example for your response.

1. **Prompt:** When might you use a *cylinder* at home?

   Personal Example:____

   ____

   ____

   ____

2. **Prompt:** Tell me about a time that you had to *compare* two things.

   Personal Example:____

   ____

   ____

   ____

3. **Prompt:** Describe an experience you have had using a *cube*.

   Personal Example:____

   ____

   ____

   ____

4. **Prompt:** What is an object in your home that has a shape of a *sphere*?

   Personal Example:____

   ____

   ____

   ____

Equivalents in Fractions

Featured Academic Vocabulary Strategies

- **Cloze Sentences:** Developing Oral Language (page 14)
- **Vocabulary Diagram:** Teaching Words (page 24)

Standards

- **McREL:** Students will understand the concepts related to fractions and decimals.
- **McREL:** Students will understand level-appropriate sight words and vocabulary.
- **TESOL:** Students will use appropriate learning strategies to construct and apply academic knowledge.

Materials

- unifix cubes in two colors
- chart paper
- *Drawing Fractions* (page 105)
- *Vocabulary Diagram: Fraction* (page 106)
- *Fraction Word Translations* (page 107)

Focus Vocabulary Words	
Specialized Content Vocabulary	**General Academic Vocabulary**
denominator fraction numerator simplify equivalent	equal

Procedure

1. Begin the lesson by reviewing with students what they already know about *fractions*. Use two different colored unifix cubes to show $\frac{3}{4}$. Ask students to share how many there are of each color. As a group, represent the total of each colored cube by writing two fractions. For example, connect 3 red cubes and 1 blue cube and say, "Three-fourths of these cubes are red. One-fourth of the cubes are blue." Use a sheet of chart paper to record the fractions $\frac{1}{4}$ and $\frac{3}{4}$. Then use these examples to help teach the focus vocabulary words. Point out the *numerator* and *denominator* of each fraction.
2. Take the unifix cubes to show $\frac{6}{8}$. Use the same colors and proportions as you did for $\frac{3}{4}$. Explain to students that: Six-eighths of the cubes are red and two-eighths of the cubes are blue.
3. Place the two fraction examples next to each other. Ask students to talk about how $\frac{3}{4}$ and $\frac{6}{8}$ are similar. Use these examples to discuss the terms *simplify*, *equal*, and *equivalent*.
4. Use the **Cloze Sentences** strategy (page 14) to reinforce students' knowledge of the new vocabulary.

Procedure *(cont.)*

Some examples of cloze sentences include the following:

- The ________ shows the number of parts that make up the whole. *(denominator)*
- In order to study a ________, you have to know that it is not a whole number. *(fraction)*
- The ________ is written above the line of a fraction. *(numerator)*
- ________ fractions have the same value. *(equivalent)*

5. Distribute copies of the *Drawing Fractions* activity sheet (page 105) to students. Tell students that they are going to represent the equivalent fractions with pictures. Encourage them to show how the fractions are related by drawing a similar picture.
6. When students are finished with their activity sheets, have them share their pictures in pairs. Review the work as a group.
7. Use the **Vocabulary Diagram** strategy (page 24) with students. Explain to students that they will be analyzing the vocabulary word *fraction*.
8. Distribute copies of the *Vocabulary Diagram: Fraction* activity sheet (page 106) to students. Tell students that completing these activity sheets is going to be a way for them to learn even more about the new vocabulary they have been studying.
9. Distribute copies of the *Fraction Word Translations* assessment sheet (page 107) to students. Have students complete the assessment individually to determine whether they understand how to correctly use vocabulary in more basic ways than proper, academic contexts.

Differentiation

English language support—Use objects, pictures, and numbers to help students learn more about fractions. Pick examples that are relevant to students' lives and experiences.

Below-level Students—Work with students in creating illustrations of additional equivalent fractions. Have students label their fractions.

Above-level students—Have students write their own cloze sentences using the focus vocabulary and then share their sentences in pairs.

Name________________________________

Drawing Fractions

DIRECTIONS Fill in each box below with pictures that prove that the two fractions are equivalent.

$\frac{1}{2}$ =	$\frac{2}{4}$

$\frac{3}{4}$ =	$\frac{9}{12}$

$\frac{2}{3}$ =	$\frac{6}{9}$

Name________________________________

Vocabulary Diagram: Fraction

Record your responses for the word *fraction*. Write your answers below.

Word:	**Synonyms:** **Antonyms:**
Other Forms of the Word:	**Example:**
Picture:	**Sentence:** ______________________ ______________________ ______________________ ______________________ ______________________ ______________________

Name________________________________

Fraction Word Translations

Read each original sentence below. Then translate each sentence from academic language into casual language.

1. **Original sentence:** The *denominators* of the two fractions were different even though they were *equivalent* in value.

   Student sentence: ________________________________

   ____

   ____

2. **Original sentence:** A *numerator* of a *fraction* is always written on top of the denominator.

   Student sentence: ________________________________

   ____

   ____

3. **Original sentence:** Just because the numerators are *equal*, does not mean the *fractions* are equal.

   Student sentence: ________________________________

   ____

   ____

4. **Original sentence:** A *fraction* is written with both a *numerator* and a *denominator.*

   Student sentence: ________________________________

   ____

   ____

Adding Decimals

Featured Academic Vocabulary Strategies

- **Mystery Bag:** Developing Oral Language (page 8)
- **Vocabulary Journal:** Independent Word Learning (page 28)

Standards

- **McREL:** Students will solve word problems and real-world problems involving number operations, including those that specify units.
- **McREL:** Students will use level-appropriate vocabulary in speech.
- **TESOL:** Students will use appropriate learning strategies to construct and apply academic knowledge.

Materials

- items to represent vocabulary words
- paper bags filled with coins per student pairs
- *Picking Coins* (page 110)
- *Decimal Word Reflections* (page 111)
- *Decimal Context Completion* (page 112)

Focus Vocabulary Words	
Specialized Content Vocabulary	**General Academic Vocabulary**
calculate cent decimal dollar	coin

Procedure

1. Before beginning this lesson, gather one item to represent each of the selected vocabulary words and place them in a paper bag. For example, a coin can represent *cent*, a dollar bill can represent *dollar*, and a calculator can represent *calculate*.
2. Begin the lesson by using the **Mystery Bag** strategy (page 8) to develop students' oral language, activate their prior knowledge, and generate interest in the lesson topic.
3. Review with students each *coin* name and value in *decimals*. Distribute copies of the *Picking Coins* activity sheet (page 110) to students. Place students in pairs. Distribute paper bags and coins to student pairs. Explain to them that they will be picking coins out of the bag three times. Each draw will be recorded on the sheet, and then students will be working together to add the two amounts together to calculate a total.

Procedure *(cont.)*

4. Model for students how to record money amounts by including a decimal. Encourage students to grab a big handful of coins rather than just a small amount. Tell students that they will be doing this three times. Give them time to work in pairs to complete their work on the activity sheet.

5. Use the **Vocabulary Journal** strategy (page 28) with students to remind them of the importance of having a place to routinely write about and reflect on vocabulary words that they are learning.

6. Distribute copies of the *Decimal Word Reflections* activity sheet (page 111) to students. Tell students that these sheets are going to become a part of their vocabulary journals. Using the activity sheet, tell students to record information about the word *decimal*. Have students share their word reflections when they are finished.

7. Distribute copies of the *Decimal Context Completion* assessment sheet (page 112) to students. Have students complete the assessment individually to determine whether they understand how to use new vocabulary correctly in meaningful contexts.

Differentiation

English language support—Use a calculator to further explain the word *calculate*. Talk about how to use a calculator and how the tool can do the same types of operations that students can solve themselves.

Below-level students—Have students complete the activity sheets in small groups to monitor students' work and provide assistance.

Above-level students—Have students practice decimal subtraction. Show students that they can use the two amounts they pick on the *Picking Coins* activity sheet to practice their subtractions skills, too.

Name________________________________

Picking Coins

DIRECTIONS Fill in the chart below by selecting coins from the bag your teacher gave you. Record the amount of money you select. Do it again. Then add the two amounts and show your answer in the space below. Do this three times.

	Number of Quarters	Number of Dimes	Number of Nickels	Number of Pennies	Total Amount in dollars and cents
1st Pick					.
2nd Pick					.
				Total of Both Picks	.

	Number of Quarters	Number of Dimes	Number of Nickels	Number of Pennies	Total Amount in dollars and cents
1st Pick					.
2nd Pick					.
				Total of Both Picks	.

	Number of Quarters	Number of Dimes	Number of Nickels	Number of Pennies	Total Amount in dollars and cents
1st Pick					.
2nd Pick					.
				Total of Both Picks	.

Name________________________________

Decimal Word Reflections

Write the word *decimal* in the box below. Then draw a picture of the word and write a definition of the word. Finally, write a sentence that uses the word correctly.

Word:

Picture:

Definition: ____

____

____

Sentence: ____

____

____

Name________________________________

Decimal Context Completion

DIRECTIONS Read each context completion sentence starter. Fill in the blank with information that correctly completes the sentence.

1. **Sentence starter:** A *cent* and a *dollar* are related because ____________________

____

____

2. **Sentence starter:** A *decimal point* is needed when solving a problem using money because ____________________

____

____

3. **Sentence starter:** One way to *calculate* the amount of money you have is to ____________________

____

____

4. **Sentence starter:** Solving a word problem using *cents* requires a *decimal point* because ____________________

____

____

Understanding the Water Cycle

Featured Academic Vocabulary Strategies

- **Have You Ever?:** Developing Oral Language (page 10)
- **Vocabulary Diagram:** Teaching Words (page 24)

Standards

- **McREL:** Students will know that water exists in the air in different forms and changes from one form to another through various processes.
- **McREL:** Students will use level-appropriate vocabulary in speech.
- **TESOL:** Students will use learning strategies to extend their communicative competence.

Materials

- *Experiences with the Water Cycle* (page 115)
- crayons, colored pencils, or markers
- *Vocabulary Diagram: Water Cycle* (page 116)
- *Water Cycle Context Completion* (page 117)

Focus Vocabulary Words	
Specialized Content Vocabulary	**General Academic Vocabulary**
condensation evaporation precipitation	cycle

Procedure

1. Begin the lesson by describing the water *cycle* with students. Draw a diagram as you discuss with students the parts of the water cycle.
2. For each process that is depicted on the water cycle, have students brainstorm examples that they are already familiar with from their own lives and experiences. For example, a student may comment that *evaporation* occurs when his or her mom boils water at home and the hot water produces steam. Another student may comment that he or she notices *condensation* on cold mornings when there is dew on the ground.
3. Use the **Have You Ever?** strategy (page 10) to connect students' knowledge of the concepts to their own personal experiences. The following are some examples to discuss with students:
    - When was the last time you felt *precipitation*?
    - Describe a time when you saw something *evaporate*.
    - What are some other reoccurring cycles you know of?

Procedure *(cont.)*

4. Distribute copies of the *Experiences with the Water Cycle* activity sheet (page 115) to students. Explain that they will be drawing a picture that shows a personal experience they have had and is related to the new vocabulary they are studying. Provide students with crayons, colored pencils, or markers to help them complete their pictures. Ask them to share their ideas orally in pairs when they are finished.
5. Use the **Vocabulary Diagram** strategy (page 24) with students and discuss how examining unfamiliar words will deepen their understanding.
6. Distribute copies of the *Vocabulary Diagram: Water Cycle* activity sheet (page 116) to students. Tell students that they will select one of the specialized content vocabulary words to further examine. When students are done with the activity page, have student volunteers share their findings.
7. Distribute copies of the *Water Cycle Context Completion* assessment sheet (page 117) to students. Have students complete the assessment individually to determine whether they understand how to correctly use context to write meaningful sentences with the newly learned specialized content and the general academic vocabulary.

Differentiation

- **English language support**—Provide simpler sentence frames for students to complete as the vocabulary words are discussed.
- **Below-level students**—As the water cycle is being explained, share examples and information that is relevant to students' lives so that students can begin to build their own connections.
- **Above-level students**—Have students write a short explanation of the water cycle. Encourage them to add illustrations to their explanations.

Name ______________________________

Experiences with the Water Cycle

DIRECTIONS Choose one process from the water cycle that you learned about. Draw and label a picture that shows what the process may look like in the real world. Then answer the questions below.

1. What process did you draw in the box above?

____

2. Describe the process by using new vocabulary words that you have learned.

____

____

____

3. Write about a personal connection you have to this part of the water cycle.

____

____

____

Name________________________________

Vocabulary Diagram: Water Cycle

DIRECTIONS Select a vocabulary word you learned about. Record your responses below.

Word:	**Synonyms:** **Antonyms:**
Other Forms of the Word:	**Example:**
Picture:	**Sentence:** ____________________ ____________________ ____________________ ____________________ ____________________ ____________________

Name________________________________

Water Cycle Context Completion

DIRECTIONS Read each Context Completion sentence starter. Fill in the blank with information that correctly completes the sentence.

1. **Sentence starter:** The water *cycle* is continuous because ______________

____

____

____

2. **Sentence starter:** *Condensation* is the *process* of______________

____

____

____

3. **Sentence starter:** One way to *measure precipitation* is to ______________

____

____

____

4. **Sentence starter:** The *process* of *evaporation* happens when ______________

____

____

____

The Solar System

Featured Academic Vocabulary Strategies

- **Alike and Different:** Developing Oral Language (page 16)
- **Ten Important Words:** Developing Word Consciousness (page 20)

Standards

- **McREL:** Students will know that Earth is one of several planets that orbit the sun and that the moon orbits Earth.
- **McREL:** Students will use skills and strategies to read a variety of literary texts.
- **TESOL:** Students will use English to obtain, process, construct, and provide subject-matter information in spoken and written form.

Materials

- pictures of planets
- *Earth and the Moon* (page 120)
- *Parts of the Solar System* (page 121)
- *Solar System Context Interpretation* (page 122)
- sticky notes
- chart paper
- marker

Focus Vocabulary Words	
Specialized Content Vocabulary	**General Academic Vocabulary**
moon orbit planet	identify

Procedure

1. Begin the lesson by reviewing with students what they know about the solar system. Show students pictures of planets to activate background knowledge. Review the *planets* and the order in which they are from the sun (Mercury, Venus, Earth, Mars, Jupiter, Saturn, Uranus, Neptune).
2. Share the vocabulary words with students. Continue to use the picture to discuss those terms and share the definitions of all the vocabulary words. For example, students can be told that to be able to *identify* a planet means to recognize it and recall its name.
3. Use the **Alike and Different** strategy (page 16) to help students make connections among words and deepen their understanding of new vocabulary.
4. Write the vocabulary pair *moon* and *planet* on the board. Ask students to think about what they know about each of these words. Then ask students to discuss how these words are similar and different.
5. Record student ideas on a Venn diagram on the board. Remind students how to properly fill out the diagram.

Procedure *(cont.)*

6. Explain to students that Earth *orbits* the sun, and the moon orbits the Earth. Tell students that it takes about 27 days for the moon to go around or orbit Earth and 365 days or a year for Earth to orbit the sun.

7. Distribute copies of the *Earth and the Moon* activity sheet (page 120) to students. Tell students that they will be completing a Venn diagram as a class, similar to the one that was discussed earlier in this lesson. This time students will be focusing on the planet Earth and the moon and writing similarities and differences between both. Complete the diagram as a class.

8. Use the **Ten Important Words** strategy (page 20) with students and remind them of the importance of recognizing new and interesting vocabulary in science texts. Tell students that they will be looking for the ten most important words in a reading passage. Some of the words they find may be the same as the focus vocabulary words, and some may be different.

9. Distribute copies of the *Parts of the Solar System* activity sheet (page 121) to students. Show students that they will record their ten words on this sheet. When students are finished, give them time to share their findings in pairs and to write their words on sticky notes to analyze students' findings as a class.

10. Distribute copies of the *Solar System Context Interpretation* assessment sheet (page 122) to students. Have students complete the assessment individually to determine whether they understand how to correctly use the focus vocabulary words within an appropriate context.

Differentiation

- **English language support**—Have students include illustrations to their Venn diagrams as visuals.
- **Below-level students**—Have students work as a small group to read the passage, record important vocabulary, and write a summary.
- **Above-level students**—Have students fill out the Venn diagrams independently. Give each student a different word pair. Then ask students to share their work with their classmates.

Name________________________________

Earth and the Moon

DIRECTIONS Look at the Venn diagram below. Think about how Earth and the moon are similar and different. Write your notes below as they are discussed in class.

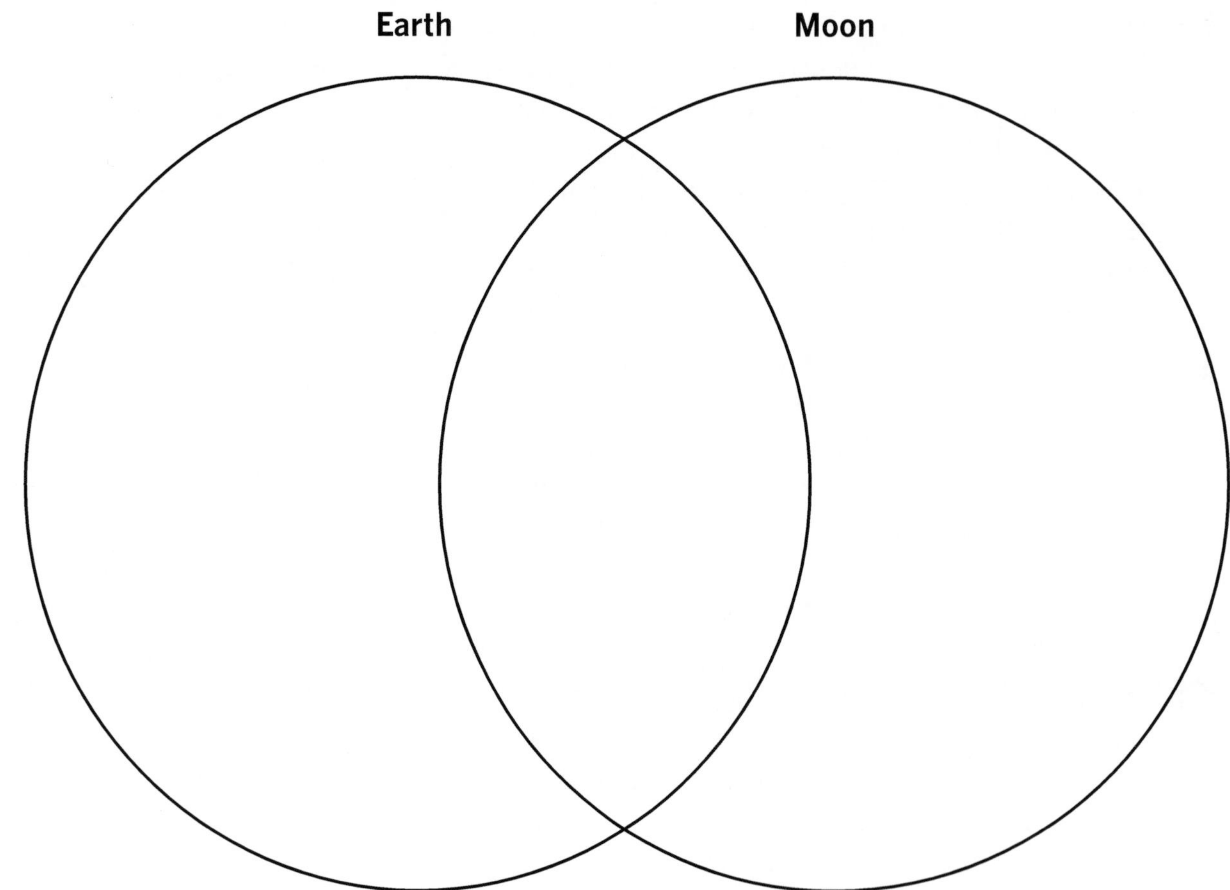

DIRECTIONS Use the Word Box below to fill in the blanks.

Word Box	
moon	orbits
year	sun

Earth ______________________ the sun and the ______________________ orbits Earth. It takes about 27 days for the moon to orbit Earth and 365 days or a ______________________ for Earth to orbit the ______________________.

Name________________________________

Parts of the Solar System

DIRECTIONS Read the passage below. Look for 10 words you think are important about our solar system. Circle your words in the reading passage and then write them in the boxes below.

Our solar system is an exciting place. Some objects in space consist of the sun and eight planets. Our solar system is over 4.6 billion years old!

The sun is a middle-size yellow star that scientists have named Sol. This is why we refer to our system of planets as the Solar System. During periods of high solar activity, the sun commonly releases massive amounts of gas and plasma.

In our solar system, there are eight planets that orbit the sun. The eight planets travel in a counter clockwise direction. Mercury, Venus, Earth, and Mars are the planets closest to the sun. They are known as the inner planets. Jupiter, Saturn, Uranus, and Neptune are farthest from the sun. They are known as the outer planets.

There are many other objects in our solar system, but knowing that there are eight planets and the sun already makes the solar system a fascinating place!

Important Words:	

Name ____________________

Solar System Context Interpretation

DIRECTIONS Read each sentence below. Then read the question and write your answer.

1. **Context:** A long time ago scientists were finally able to *identify* other planets.

   Question: How did the scientists feel?

   Response: ____________________

   ____

2. **Context:** The family was able to watch a rare blue *moon* light up the night sky.

   Question: How did the family feel?

   Response: ____________________

   ____

3. **Context:** The people enjoyed watching a video clip of the planets *orbiting in space*.

   Question: How did the people feel?

   Response: ____________________

   ____

4. **Context:** The girl saw an exciting picture of astronauts looking down on *Earth*.

   Question: How did the girl feel?

   Response: ____________________

   ____

Adapting for Survival

Featured Academic Vocabulary Strategies

- **Idea Completions:** Developing Oral Language (page 18)
- **Content Links:** Teaching Words (page 26)

Standards

- **McREL:** Students will know that living organisms have distinct structures and body systems serve specific functions in growth, survival, and reproduction.
- **McREL:** Students will use level-appropriate vocabulary in speech.
- **TESOL:** Students will use English to obtain, process, construct, and provide subject-matter information in spoken and written form.

Materials

- photographs depicting animal adaptations
- *Adaptations in Nature* (page 125)
- index cards
- *Connecting to What You Know* (page 126)
- *Yes-No-Why?: Survival* (page 127)

Focus Vocabulary Words	
Specialized Content Vocabulary	**General Academic Vocabulary**
adaptation animals environment habitat plants	detect

Procedure

1. Begin the lesson by discussing what *plants* and *animals* need in order to survive in the wild. Record students' responses.
2. Discuss how animals will develop *adaptations* to survive and thrive in their natural *environments*. Talk about examples of adaptations, and show pictures to students. Some examples may include a porcupine's quills, a spider's web, or an insect's camouflage.
3. As you continue to introduce these concepts to students, use the **Idea Completions** strategy (page 18) to develop students' oral language. Some examples of idea completions include the following:
   - The animal's natural *habitat* is a place where…
   - Some *plants* such as the cactus have special adaptations such as...
   - An example of an animal being able to sense and *detect* something is…
   - An example of an animal's home or *environment* is...

Procedure *(cont.)*

4. Distribute copies of the *Adaptations in Nature* activity sheet (page 125) to students. Tell students that they will each write about a plant or animal that uses an adaptation to help it survive in the wild. Students may work in pairs, small groups, or independently.
5. Have student volunteers share their pictures and writing with the whole group. Facilitate a whole-class discussion about the survival of animals and plants due to adaptations. Then have students brainstorm additional words they learned as a result of the lesson. End the list when there is one word for every student in the class.
6. Record the words on index cards and distribute one card to each student. Complete the **Content Links** strategy (page 26) with students to solidify their comprehension of the words.
7. Distribute copies of the *Connecting to What You Know* activity sheet (page 126) to students. Have students complete the activity sheet.
8. Distribute copies of the *Yes-No-Why?: Survival* assessment sheet (page 127) to students. Have students complete the assessment individually to determine whether they understand each word definition and how the words are used in real-world applications.

Differentiation

English language support—Write sentence frames for your Idea Completions sentences with your students' prior knowledge and background experience in mind.

Below-level students—Allow students to conduct research in pairs or small groups. Supervise their progress and help them find appropriate materials to use to complete their work.

Above-level students—Ask students to pair words in multiple ways and explain the relationships between and among words.

Name________________________________

Adaptations in Nature

DIRECTIONS Fill in the boxes below with information that you learned about your adaptation.

My plant or animal is:

____

Its adaptation is:

____

____

The adaptation helps the plant or animal to:

____

____

____

Here is a picture of the adaptation:

Name________________________________

Connecting to What You Know

DIRECTIONS Write the words you linked in the spaces below. Then write a short description of how the words are linked and how these two words are connected to what you have learned about adaptations.

Word 1	Word 2
______________________	______________________

These words are linked because....

____

____

____

____

These words are related to what I know about adaptations in nature because...

____

____

____

____

____

____

____

____

____

____

____

Name________________________________

Yes-No-Why?: Survival

DIRECTIONS Read each sentence below. Think about whether the context makes sense. Then write your response. Use the following sentence stems to begin your sentence:

- This makes sense because...
- This does not make sense because...
- This seems logical because...
- This seems illogical because...

1. **Sentence:** An *animal* may develop an *adaptation* over time to protect itself from other animals.

   Response: ____

   ____

   ____

2. **Sentence:** All *plants* and *animals* belong to an *environment*.

   Response: ____

   ____

   ____

3. **Sentence:** *Animals* cannot *detect* prey in cold climates.

   Response: ____

   ____

   ____

4. **Sentence:** The ways that humans interact with an animal's *habitat* will impact its ability to survive.

   Response: ____

   ____

   ____

Solid, Liquid, or Gas?

Featured Academic Vocabulary Strategies

- **Mystery Bag:** Developing Oral Language (page 8)
- **Clue Hunt:** Independent Word Learning (page 30)

Standards

- **McREL:** Students will know that matter has different states and that each state has distinct physical properties.
- **McREL:** Students will use level-appropriate vocabulary in speech.
- **TESOL:** Students will use English to obtain, process, construct, and provide subject-matter information in spoken and written form.

Materials

- numerous items representing the different states of matter
- paper bag
- *Different States of Matter* (page 130)
- *Searching for Clues* (page 131)
- *Show You Know About States of Matter* (page 132)

Focus Vocabulary Words	
Specialized Content Vocabulary	**General Academic Vocabulary**
gas liquid solid states of matter	property

Procedure

1. Before beginning this lesson, gather one item to represent each of the selected vocabulary words and place them in a paper bag. For example, an ice cube can represent *solid*, an empty resealable bag trapped with air can represent *gas*, and a jar filled with water can represent *liquid*.
2. Begin the lesson by using the **Mystery Bag** strategy (page 8) to develop students' oral language, activate their prior knowledge, and generate interest in the lesson topic. Show students the items for this activity.
3. Review with students each vocabulary word and definition. Briefly discuss examples of each word, such as the following:
   - Steam is a type of *gas*.
   - Water can be in different *states of matter*.
   - Liquids share the same *properties*.

Procedure *(cont.)*

4. Distribute copies of the *Different States of Matter* activity sheet (page 130) to students. Explain to students that they will be seeing different objects, and that they are going to have to decide if each object is a gas, solid, or liquid. Have students complete the activity sheet as a class. Show students the remaining items representing the different properties.

5. Discuss how students categorized each item. Discuss the properties and what they have in common. Have students record their ideas at the bottom of the activity sheets. Are there any items that were not universally accepted as one state of matter or another? Some items may be obvious, while other items may spark a debate. For example, is jelly a solid or a liquid? What about ice cream? Give students time to share their arguments for why certain items have different properties.

6. Use the **Clue Hunt** strategy (page 30) with students and discuss how context clues can be an essential tool for understanding new and unfamiliar vocabulary. Review with students what context clues are.

7. Distribute copies of the *Searching for Clues* activity sheet (page 131) to students. Tell students that these sheets will provide a place for students to record the context clues they find as they read a passage related to the topic. Have students work in pairs to read the passage and complete their activity sheets.

8. Distribute copies of the *Show You Know About States of Matter* assessment sheet (page 132) to students. Have students complete the assessment individually to determine whether they understand how to correctly use the specialized content and the general academic vocabulary in context.

Differentiation

English language support—Read the text aloud to students and check for comprehension while reading. Help students find the context clues and complete their activity sheets.

Below-level students—Provide students with clear examples of each type of context clue. Write them on a worksheet for students to use as a reference while they read the passage.

Above-level students—Ask students to research additional materials at home to add to their *Different States of Matter* activity sheet. Have them share what they have added with the class.

Name________________________________

Different States of Matter

DIRECTIONS Your teacher will show you some objects. Is it a *solid*, a *gas*, or a *liquid*? Pick a category for each material and record it in the chart below.

Solid	Gas	Liquid

1. What is a *property* of a *liquid*?

____

____

2. What is a *property* of a *gas*?

____

____

3. What is a *property* of a *solid*?

____

____

Name________________________________

Searching for Clues

DIRECTIONS Read the passage. Complete the table below by finding context clues in the reading passage.

How can you tell if something is a solid, a liquid, or a gas? It is helpful if you closely examine the substance and think of how it compares with other substances you know.

Which property, or characteristic, does it share with another substance? Does it flow and take the shape of its container? Then it must be a liquid. Some substances have a distinct shape and are not easily transformed. This type of substance is known as a solid. A gas, on the other hand, has no fixed shape and can expand indefinitely.

Solid, liquid, and gas are examples of different states of matter. These distinct forms of matter are better understood when you consider all the different kinds of substances that belong in each category and the properties that they share. What types of solids, liquids, and gases do you use in your own life?

Words	Context Clues in Text
property	
liquid	
solid	
gas	

Name________________________________

Show You Know About States of Matter

DIRECTIONS Read each pair of vocabulary words. Then write a sentence that uses the words appropriately in context.

1. **Vocabulary words:** *gas, solid*

   Student response: ____

   ____

   ____

2. **Vocabulary words:** *states of matter, property*

   Student response: ____

   ____

   ____

3. **Vocabulary words:** *liquid, states of matter*

   Student response: ____

   ____

   ____

4. **Vocabulary words:** *solid, property*

   Student response: ____

   ____

   ____

5. **Vocabulary words:** *gas, liquid*

   Student response: ____

   ____

   ____

Scientific Investigations

Featured Academic Vocabulary Strategies

- **Cloze Sentences:** Developing Oral Language (page 14)
- **Vocabulary Journal:** Independent Word Learning (page 28)

Standards

- **McREL:** Students will plan and conduct simple investigations.
- **McREL:** Students will use level-appropriate vocabulary in speech.
- **TESOL:** Students will use English to obtain, process, construct, and provide subject-matter information in spoken and written form.

Materials

- chart paper
- marker
- *Investigation Work* (page 135)
- *Analyzing the Investigation* (page 136)
- *Personal Examples About Scientific Investigations* (page 137)

Focus Vocabulary Words	
Specialized Content Vocabulary	**General Academic Vocabulary**
hypothesis investigation testable question	data observe procedure

Procedure

1. Begin the lesson by telling students that they are going to be practicing designing their own science *investigation*. Use a sheet of chart paper to make a checklist of the steps required to complete an investigation. They may include the following:
   - Write a *testable question*, or a *hypothesis*.
   - Write an educated guess to your question.
   - *Observe* and collect *data*.
   - Draw logical conclusions based on your data.
2. As you write the checklist together, discuss the focus vocabulary words and how they relate to the overall topic of science investigations.
3. Use the **Cloze Sentences** strategy (page 14) to reinforce students' knowledge of the new vocabulary and to give them an opportunity to share their ideas orally. Some examples of cloze sentences include the following:
   - Information and facts gathered in science are also known as ________. *(data)*

Procedure *(cont.)*

- Being aware and noticing things around you makes for a careful ________. *(observation)*
- If you do not follow the ________ exactly as the steps are listed, you may not complete the experiment correctly. *(procedure)*
- A ________ can be answered by designing and conducting an experiment. *(hypothesis)*

4. Distribute copies of the *Investigation Work* activity sheet (page 135) to students and explain that as a class they will be using this sheet to record information about an investigation that they would like to design. Review the activity sheet with students. Then as a class complete the activity sheet based on a scientific investigation students would like to create.

5. Use the **Vocabulary Journal** strategy (page 28) with students to remind them of the importance of having a place to routinely write about and reflect on vocabulary words. Have each student create an entry for a focus vocabulary word from this lesson. Have them write about how this word relates to the simple investigation that they designed and carried out. Distribute copies of the *Analyzing the Investigation* activity sheet (page 136) for students to use to record their ideas for their journal entries.

6. Distribute copies of the *Personal Examples About Scientific Investigations* assessment sheet (page 137) to students. Have students complete the assessment individually to determine whether they understand how to correctly use the vocabulary words.

Differentiation

English language support—Allow students to also draw pictures in their journal entries. Help them label their work with the focus vocabulary words.

Below-level students—Work with students as a group on a particular investigation and guide them through all parts of the experiment. Help students record their ideas on both activity sheets.

Above-level students—Challenge students to demonstrate their understanding of new vocabulary by having them draft their own cloze sentences to share in pairs or with the group.

Name________________________________

Investigation Work

DIRECTIONS Fill out the information below about the investigation your class would like to create.

My testable question:

____

____

____

____

My hypothesis and plan for testing the testable question:

____

____

____

____

My data and observations:

____

____

____

____

My conclusions:

____

____

____

____

Name________________________________

Analyzing the Investigation

Pick a word or words from the Word Box below. Use the selected words to describe what you plan to do when you do your scientific investigation.

Word Box	
data	observation
hypothesis	procedure
investigation	testable question

____

____

____

____

____

____

____

____

____

____

____

____

____

Name________________________________

Personal Examples About Scientific Investigations

Read each prompt. Then write a personal example for your response.

1. **Prompt:** Besides during science, when might you create a *testable question* during school?

   Personal Example:________________________________

   ____

   ____

2. **Prompt:** Write about a time that an *observation* helped you better understand a situation.

   Personal Example:________________________________

   ____

   ____

3. **Prompt:** Describe a *procedure* you followed that had surprising findings at the end.

   Personal Example:________________________________

   ____

   ____

4. **Prompt:** When might you need an *investigation* to gather *data*?

   Personal Example:________________________________

   ____

   ____

Places on the Map

Featured Academic Vocabulary Strategies

- **Idea Completions:** Developing Oral Language (page 18)
- **Vocabulary Journal:** Independent Word-Learning (page 28)

Standards

- **McREL:** Students will know the basic elements of maps and globes.
- **McREL:** Students will use level-appropriate vocabulary in speech.
- **TESOL:** Students will use appropriate learning strategies to construct and apply academic knowledge.

Materials

- world map
- globe
- *Labeling a Map* (page 140)
- *Personal Connections* (page 141)
- *Show You Know About a Map* (page 142)

Focus Vocabulary Words	
Specialized Content Vocabulary	**General Academic Vocabulary**
compass rose continent globe key world map	represent

Procedure

1. Begin the lesson by showing students examples of one or more *world maps* and *globes*. As a group, talk about what they are and why people may use them. Point out features on the map and globe, including a *key* and a *compass rose*. Talk about how these two parts of a map are helpful to someone. For example, students might be told, "A *key* helps people understand what the symbols on a map mean."

2. As you introduce these concepts to students, use the **Idea Completions** strategy (page 18) to introduce the vocabulary strategy and develop students' oral language.

   Some examples of idea completions to integrate include the following:

   - A *globe represents*…
   - A *key* is a helpful part of a map because…
   - A *compass rose* diagram on a map shows…
   - One way to find a *continent* on a map is to…
   - You may notice that a *world map* includes…

Procedure *(cont.)*

3. Distribute copies of the *Labeling a Map* activity sheet (page 140) to students. Explain to students that they will be identifying and labeling key features of a world map. Review the activity sheet as a class so that students understand what they will be recording. Then give students time to complete the activity sheet. When they are finished, give students time to discuss the parts of a map that they noticed and labeled.
4. Use the **Vocabulary Journal** strategy (page 28) with students to remind them of the importance of having a place to routinely write about and reflect on vocabulary words that they are learning.
5. Distribute copies of the *Personal Connections* activity sheet (page 141) to students. Tell students that these sheets are going to be a part of their vocabulary journals. Tell students to use the sheet to record personal connections they may have to a word that they have learned about maps and globes. If possible, share your own personal connection to one of the vocabulary words.
6. Distribute copies of the *Show You Know About a Map* assessment sheet (page 142) to students. Have students complete the assessment individually to determine whether they understand how to correctly use the specialized content and the general academic vocabulary in context.

Differentiation

- **English language support—**Bring in different kinds of maps, including a state map, a city street map, and a map of a smaller location such as a park or museum. Talk with students about the reasons that people would need to use maps of different areas.
- **Below-level students—**Allow students to complete all parts of the activity sheets with a partner to have additional opportunities to discuss the vocabulary words.
- **Above-level students—**Have students sketch their own maps of the school or their neighborhood. Have them include a key and a compass rose.

Name______________________________

Labeling a Map

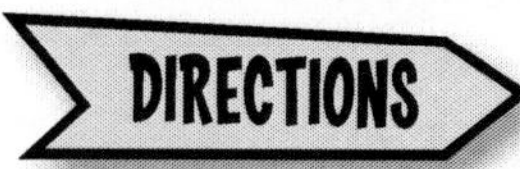

DIRECTIONS Look at the world map below. Label the different parts of the map using the words from the Word Box.

Word Box	
compass rose	ocean
continent	equator

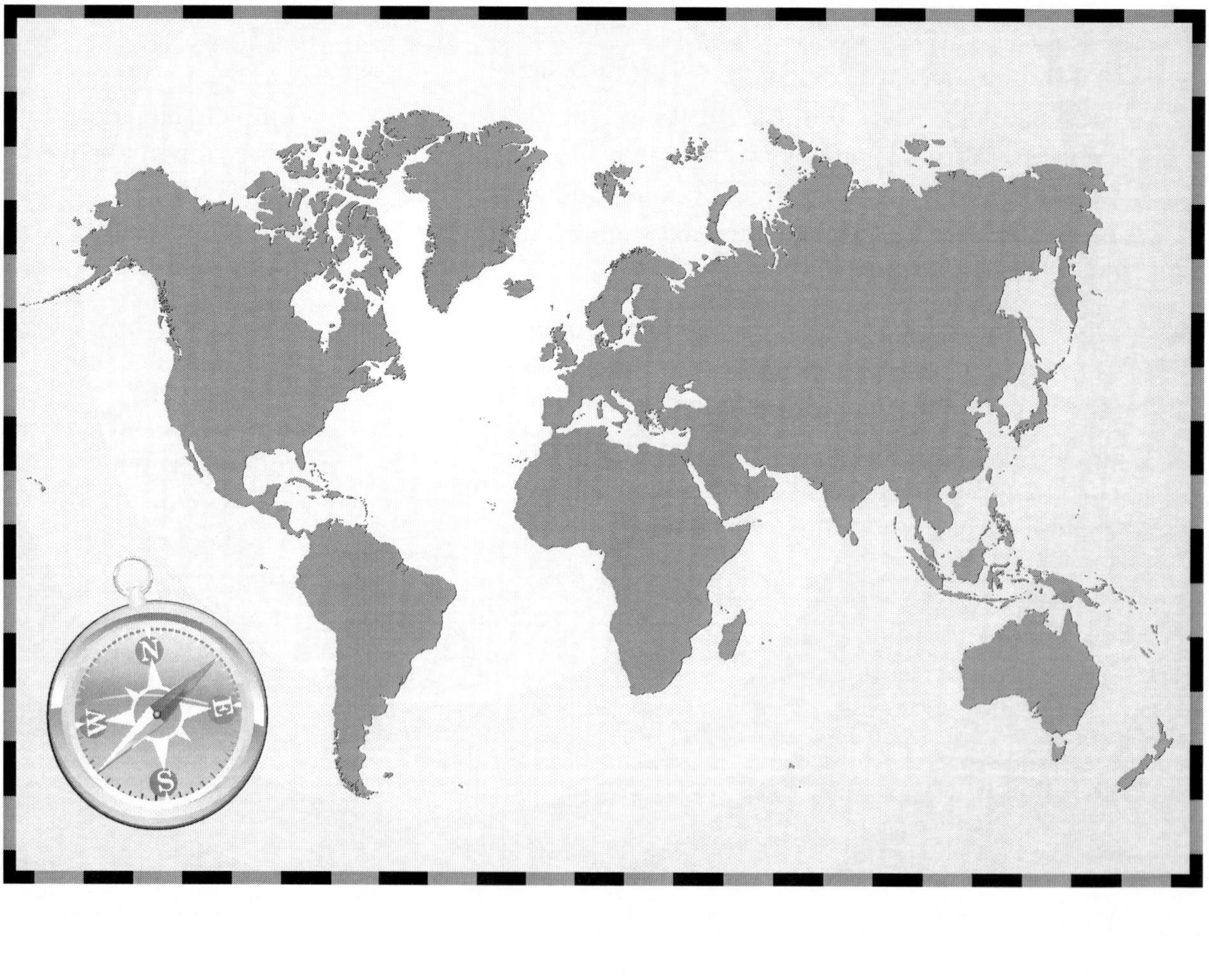

Name________________________________

Personal Connections

DIRECTIONS Look at the Word Box below. Pick two vocabulary words and write the words you have chosen in the boxes below. Then draw or write about what the words mean.

Word Box	
globe	compass rose
key	continent

Word	Word
________________	________________

These words remind me of something from my own life because...

____

____

____

____

____

____

Name________________________________

Show You Know About a Map

Read each pair of vocabulary words. Then write a sentence that uses the words appropriately in context.

1. **Vocabulary words**: *world map, globe*

   Student response: ________________________________

   ____

   ____

2. **Vocabulary words**: *map, key*

   Student response: ________________________________

   ____

   ____

3. **Vocabulary words**: *continent, globe*

   Student response: ________________________________

   ____

   ____

4. **Vocabulary words**: *key, compass rose*

   Student response: ________________________________

   ____

   ____

5. **Vocabulary words**: *compass rose, represent*

   Student response: ________________________________

   ____

   ____

Geographic Features

Featured Academic Vocabulary Strategies

- **Questions, Reasons, and Examples:** Developing Oral Language (page 12)
- **Content Links:** Teaching Words (page 26)

Standards

- **McREL:** Students will know the location of places, geographic features, and patterns of the environment.
- **McREL:** Students will respond to questions and comments.
- **TESOL:** Students will use English to obtain, process, construct, and provide subject-matter information in spoken and written form.

Materials

- pictures of geographic features
- *Pick a Feature* (page 145)
- index cards
- *Linking Ideas* (page 146)
- *Yes-No-Why?: Geographic Features* (page 147)

Focus Vocabulary Words	
Specialized Content Vocabulary	**General Academic Vocabulary**
desert forest peninsula plains	distinct feature

Procedure

1. Begin the lesson by showing students pictures of the different geographic features that represent the specialized content vocabulary words in this lesson. Ask students to share characteristics of each geographic feature. Record students' responses.
2. Review the focus vocabulary words with students. Decide how to use a visual to review and discuss these words and their definitions. For example, a student volunteer can be selected and a *feature,* such as hair, can be explained that it is a part of our bodies that distinguishes us from others.
3. Use the **Questions, Reasons, and Examples** strategy (page 12) to further discuss these vocabulary words and help students share information and examples related to these new concepts. Ask questions that students have to answer by using the vocabulary in a relevant and appropriate way.

Procedure *(cont.)*

Some examples include the following:

- What makes our classroom *distinct*?
- What are some examples of things that live in the *desert*?
- A *peninsula* is a piece of land that borders water on three sides. How is a *peninsula* different from an island?
- What are some features of the locations where you live?

4. Distribute copies of the *Pick a Feature* activity sheet (page 145) to students and explain to them that they will be depicting four geographic features to represent pictorially in the boxes. Tell students that they will also be writing information that they have learned about these features.

5. When students are finished with their work, ask them to share their ideas in pairs. Then have student volunteers share their pictures and writing with the whole group. Based on this information, help facilitate a whole-class discussion about what they know and have learned about geographic features. Then have students brainstorm additional words they learned as a result of the lesson and their research. End the list when there is one word for every student in the class.

6. Record the words on index cards and distribute one card to each student. Complete the **Content Links** strategy (page 26) with students to solidify their comprehension of the words necessary to understand the content of this lesson.

7. Distribute copies of the *Linking Ideas* activity sheet (page 146) to students. With the partner with whom they linked, have students complete the activity sheet to explain why and how their words are related.

8. Distribute copies of the *Yes-No-Why?: Geographic Features* assessment sheet (page 147) to students. Have students complete the assessment individually to see whether they understand the word definitions and how they are used in real-world applications.

Differentiation

- **English language support**—Locate videos or nature shows that focus on different geographic features. Show students what these types of regions look like around the world.
- **Below-level students**—Allow students to complete the *Pick a Feature* activity sheet with a partner, and encourage the pair to support each other's ideas and writing.
- **Above-level students**—Have students research one or more of the regions discussed in this lesson. Have students share their findings with the rest of the group.

Name________________________________

Pick a Feature

DIRECTIONS Look at the four geographic features listed in the word box below. Draw one geographic feature in each of the boxes below.

Word Box	
desert	peninsula
forest	plains

________________________ ________________________

________________________ ________________________

DIRECTIONS Write about what you learned about the four features.

____

____

____

____

____

____

Name________________________________

Linking Ideas

DIRECTIONS Write the words you linked in the spaces below and illustrate why they can be linked. Then write a short description of how and why the words are linked.

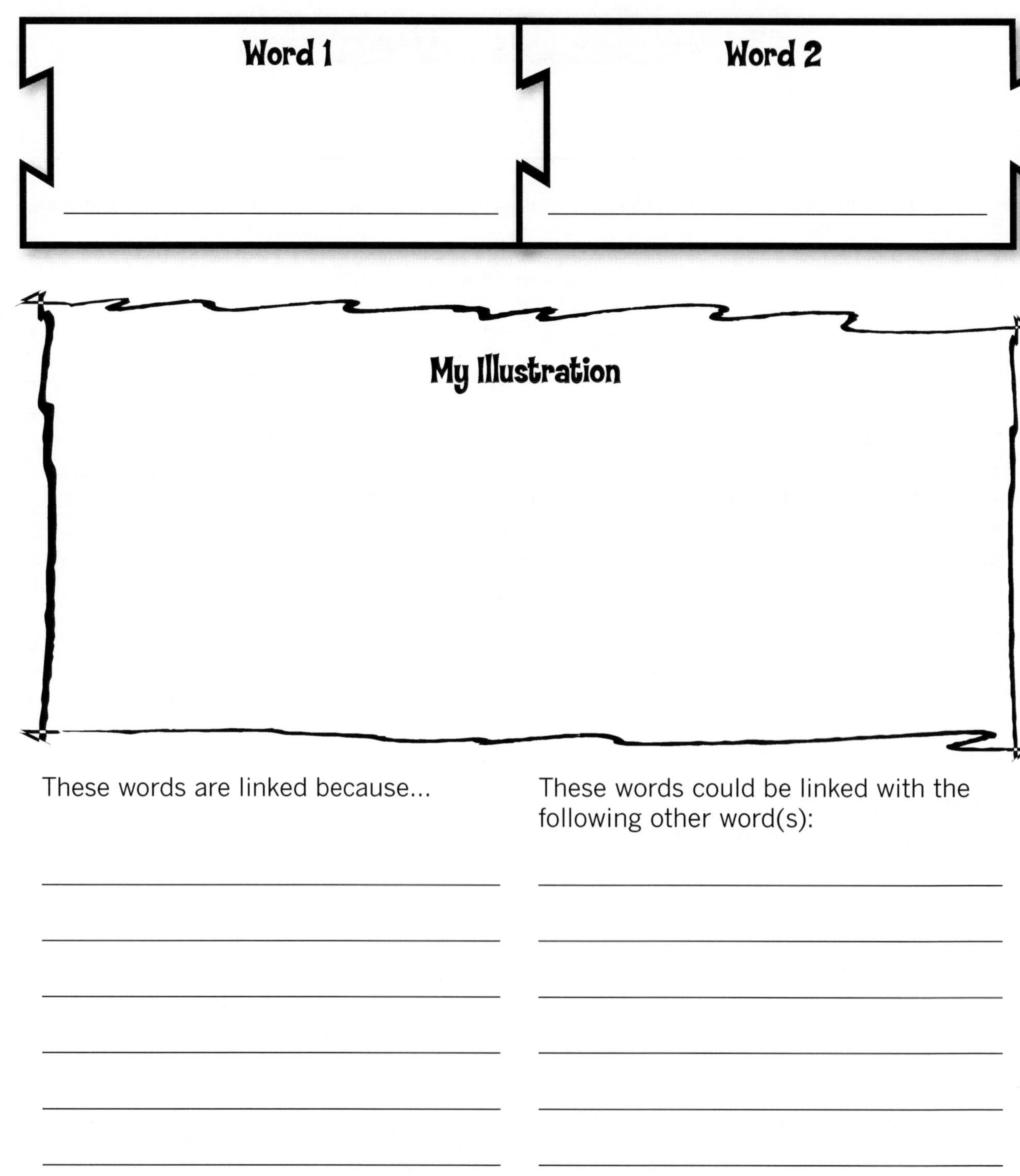

These words are linked because...

____

____

____

____

____

____

____

These words could be linked with the following other word(s):

____

____

____

____

____

____

____

Name________________________________

Yes-No-Why?: Geographic Features

DIRECTIONS Read each sentence. Think about whether the context makes sense. Then write your response. Use the following sentence stems to begin your response:

- This makes sense because...
- This does not make sense because...
- This seems logical because...
- This seems illogical because...

1. **Sentence:** A *desert* region has a unique climate and vegetation.

Response: ____

____

____

2. **Sentence:** One interesting *feature* of the *plains* is the large number of trees.

Response: ____

____

____

3. **Sentence:** A *peninsula* and an island are both surrounded by water.

Response: ____

____

____

4. **Sentence:** Scientists studying trees may want to study a *forest* or mountain region.

Response: ____

____

____

Social Studies

The Courage of Rosa Parks

Featured Academic Vocabulary Strategies

- **Alike and Different:** Developing Oral Language (page 16)
- **Vocabulary Diagram:** Teaching Words (page 24)

Standards

- **McREL:** Students will understand how people have continued to struggle to bring all groups in American society the liberties and equality promised in the basic principles of American democracy.
- **McREL:** Students will understand level-appropriate sight words and vocabulary.
- **TESOL:** Students will use English to obtain, process, construct, and provide subject-matter information in spoken and written form.

Materials

- photograph of Rosa Parks
- *Equal Rights Web* (page 150)
- *Vocabulary Diagram: Equality* (page 151)
- *Personal Examples About Equality* (page 152)

Focus Vocabulary Words	
Specialized Content Vocabulary	**General Academic Vocabulary**
boycott civil rights equal rights hero protest	equality

Procedure

1. Begin the lesson by reviewing with students what they know about the *Civil Rights* Movement and the role that Rosa Parks played in teaching people the importance of having *equal rights*. Show the class the photograph of Rosa Parks and talk about what makes her an American *hero*. Record students' responses.
2. Share the vocabulary words with students. Continue to use the example of Rosa Parks and her actions to discuss the definitions of the words.
3. Use the **Alike and Different** strategy (page 16) to help students make connections among words and deepen their understanding of the vocabulary.
4. Write the vocabulary pair *boycott* and *protest* on the board. Ask students to think about what they know about each of these words. Then ask students to discuss how these words are similar and different.

Procedure *(cont.)*

5. Record student ideas on a Venn diagram on the board. Repeat this process for other word pairs from the vocabulary list.
6. Distribute copies of the *Equal Rights Web* activity sheet (page 150) to students. Tell students that they will be brainstorming examples of how heroes fight for the equal rights of all people. Assure students that heroes can either be well known or simply everyday citizens. Have students share their ideas.
7. Use the **Vocabulary Diagram** strategy (page 24) with students. Explain that they will be analyzing their new focus vocabulary words.
8. Distribute copies of the *Vocabulary Diagram: Equality* activity sheet (page 151) to students. Tell students that the activity will be a way for them to learn even more about the vocabulary word *boycott*. Have students complete the activity individually.
9. Distribute copies of the *Personal Examples About Equality* assessment sheet (page 152) to students. Have students complete the assessment individually to determine whether they understand how to correctly apply their knowledge of the new vocabulary.

Differentiation

- **English language support—**Work with students in small groups to complete the vocabulary diagram. Use relevant examples from students' lives to make the vocabulary more meaningful.
- **Below-level students—** Complete the *Equal Rights Web* activity sheet as a small group. Have students include illustrations to their webs as a visual.
- **Above-level students—**Have students write short essays about another hero who has worked to fight for equal rights. It may be a famous person, or it may be someone in their neighborhood, school, or family. Encourage students to include the new vocabulary they have learned in this lesson.

Name________________________________

Equal Rights Web

Look at the web below. Think about different examples of ways that heroes—famous people or everyday citizens—fight for equal rights. Record your examples in the circles below.

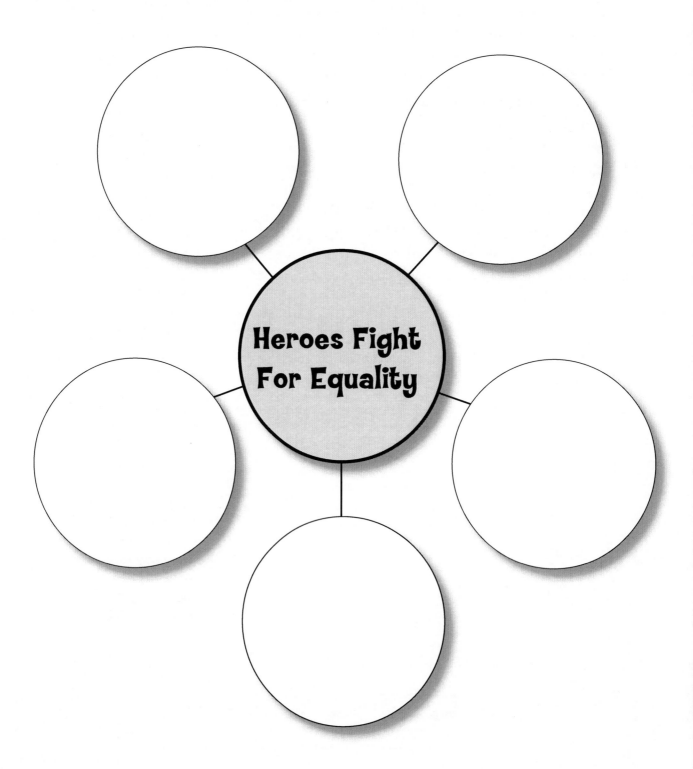

Heroes Fight For Equality

Name________________________________

Vocabulary Diagram: Equality

DIRECTIONS Record your responses for the word *boycott*. Write your answers below.

Word:	**Synonyms:** **Antonyms:**
Other Forms of the Word:	**Example:**
Picture:	**Sentence:** ____________________ ______________________ ______________________ ______________________ ______________________ ______________________

Name________________________________

Personal Examples About Equality

DIRECTIONS Read each prompt. Then write a personal example for your response.

1. **Prompt:** When might you use a *boycott* to speak out against something?

   Personal Example:____

   ____

   ____

2. **Prompt:** Describe an experience you had when you showed the qualities of a *hero.*

   Personal Example:____

   ____

   ____

3. **Prompt:** Why is *equality* and receiving *equal rights* important in your own life and experiences?

   Personal Example:____

   ____

   ____

4. **Prompt:** Tell me about something you had to *protest* recently.

   Personal Example:____

   ____

   ____

Featured Academic Vocabulary Strategies

- **Cloze Sentences:** Developing Oral Language (page 14)
- **Word Hunt:** Developing Word Consciousness (page 22)

Standards

- **McREL:** Students will understand major discoveries in science and the major scientists and inventors responsible for them.
- **McREL:** Students will use level-appropriate vocabulary in speech.
- **TESOL:** Students will use English to obtain, process, construct, and provide subject-matter information in spoken and written form.

Materials

- photograph of an early steam engine
- *Industrial Revolution* (page 155)
- *Going on a Word Hunt* (page 156)
- *Innovation Context Interpretation* (page 157)

Innovation During the Industrial Age

Focus Vocabulary Words	
Specialized Content Vocabulary	**General Academic Vocabulary**
industry innovation manufacture steam engine textile	progression

Procedure

1. Begin the lesson by reviewing with students what they know about inventions and technological innovations. Tell students that you are going to be focusing on a time in our history called the Industrial Age, occurring in the mid- to late-19th century.

2. Show students a picture of a *steam engine*. Ask students to talk about how the steam engine changed the way that people were able to do business and create factories and mills. Talk about how those changes impacted other aspects of daily life.

3. Use the **Cloze Sentences** strategy (page 14) to reinforce students' knowledge of the new vocabulary and to give them an opportunity to share their ideas orally. Some examples of cloze sentences include:

   - The textile ________ changed a great deal when cotton mills became more common. *(industry)*
   - The Industrial Revolution was a time with great ________ happening in many areas of society. *(innovation)*

Procedure *(cont.)*

4. Distribute copies of the *Industrial Revolution* activity sheet (page 155) to students and explain to them that they will be reading about the Industrial Revolution. Read the passage aloud to students and have them retell the main idea with a partner.

5. Remind students of the focus vocabulary words that they have been studying. Use the **Word Hunt** strategy (page 22) to give students a chance to locate word parts that they are studying in the *Industrial Revolution* reading passage. Review with students the word parts that are included in some of these words. Make a list of each relevant vocabulary word, the word part for which they should be looking, and the word part's definition. Example: of word parts include the following:

Word	Word Part	Definition	Related Words
innovation	*nov-*	new	innovate
manufacture	*fac-*	make, do	factory
progression	*-gress*	step	transgression
	pro-	forward	promote, project

6. Distribute copies of the *Going on a Word Hunt* activity sheet (page 156) to students and explain to them that they will be searching for the word parts from their focus vocabulary words and recording their findings on the chart. When they are finished, give students time to share the words that they located with the group.

7. Distribute copies of the *Innovation Context Interpretation* assessment sheet (page 157) to students. Have students complete the assessment individually to determine whether they understand how to use the new vocabulary words.

Differentiation

- **English language support—**Help students complete their *Word Hunt* activity sheets. If needed, underline the words containing the word parts studied during the lesson.
- **Below-level students—**Allow students to work in pairs or small groups to complete their *Going on a Word Hunt* activity sheet..
- **Above-level students—**Have students conduct their own research to find out more about the inventors behind the inventions that are discussed in this lesson.

Name________________________________

Industrial Revolution

Read the passage below. Look for and circle the vocabulary words you learned.

The Industrial Revolution was a period during the 18th and 19th centuries when many changes occurred to agriculture, manufacturing, mining, transportation, and technology. It began in the United Kingdom and eventually spread throughout Europe, North America, and eventually to the rest of the world.

The innovations occurred at such a rapid pace that as factories spread, the owners of mills, mines, and other forms of industry (especially textile manufacturers) needed large numbers of workers. In order to keep the progression of the demand moving, children were hired to work because owners knew that they could get away with paying them very low wages. Working conditions were very dangerous, and workers suffered from lack of rest, and often were not allowed time to have a meal.

Despite the hardships that people encountered during the Industrial Revolution, the innovations that occurred helped accelerate our economy and it affected the way people lived then and now.

Name________________________________

Going on a Word Hunt

DIRECTIONS Read *The Industrial Revolution*. When you are done reading, go back and do a Word Hunt for the words *innovation, manufacture*, and *progression*. Use this page to record the word part and definition to your findings.

Word	Word Part	Definition
innovation		
manufacture		
progression		

DIRECTIONS Look at your findings above. What are some related words you can think of that have the word parts listed?

____

____

____

____

____

____

____

____

____

____

____

Name________________________________

Innovation Context Interpretation

DIRECTIONS Read the sentence that uses the vocabulary word. Then read the question and write your answer.

1. **Context:** She thought it was a huge accomplishment for the *industry* to keep producing many clothing pieces.

   Question: How did she feel?

   Response: ____

   ____

2. **Context:** The cobbler was able to *manufacture* a new kind of shoe.

   Question: What did people think about this?

   Response: ____

   ____

3. **Context:** The scientist shared his *innovation*—a new device made to reduce air pollution from cars.

   Question: How did others feel about what the scientist has done?

   Response: ____

   ____

4. **Context:** The teacher noticed the *progression* that his students made in both reading and writing skills.

   Question: How did the teacher feel about this?

   Response: ____

   ____

Camel Caravans

Featured Academic Vocabulary Strategies

- **Have You Ever?:** Developing Oral Language (page 10)
- **Ten Important Words:** Developing Word Consciousness (page 20)

Standards

- **McREL:** Students will understand the development of extensive road systems.
- **McREL:** Students will understand level-appropriate vocabulary in speech.
- **TESOL:** Students will use English to obtain, process, construct, and provide subject-matter information in spoken and written form.

Materials

- *Facts About Camel Caravans* (page 160)
- *Essential Vocabulary* (page 161)
- *Camel Caravans Context Completion* (page 162)

Focus Vocabulary Words	
Specialized Content Vocabulary	**General Academic Vocabulary**
ancient caravan cargo transportation	benefit

Procedure

1. Review with students what they know about camel *caravans*, *ancient* trade routes, and *transportation* in North Africa in ancient times.
2. Continue to discuss the topic and teach the focus vocabulary words using the **Have You Ever?** strategy (page 10) to connect students' knowledge of the concepts to their own personal experiences. The following are examples to include in the discussion:
   - What do you picture in your mind when you think about *ancient* times?
   - When might you be a part of a *caravan*?
   - Describe a time when you had *cargo* that you transported from one place to another.
   - Name one *benefit* of going to school every day.
   - What kinds of *transportation* have you used in the past week?

Procedure *(cont.)*

3. Distribute copies of the *Facts About Camel Caravans* activity sheet (page 160) to students and explain to them that they will be reading about camel caravans. Point out the different categories of information that students should be looking for: *Benefits, Cargo, Difficulties,* and *Effects.* Have students work independently in completing the activity sheet, and when they are done review findings as a class.

4. Use the **Ten Important Words** strategy (page 20) with students and remind them of the importance of recognizing new and interesting vocabulary in social studies texts. Tell students they will be looking back through the *Facts About Camel Caravans* reading passage for ten words they think are important for this lesson topic. Remind students that some of the words they find may be the same as the vocabulary words, and some may be different.

5. Distribute copies of the *Essential Vocabulary* activity sheet (page 161) to students. Show students that they will record their ten words and their summaries on this sheet. When students are finished, give them time to share their writing in pairs.

6. Distribute copies of the *Camel Caravans Context Completion* assessment sheet (page 162) to students. Have students complete the assessment individually to determine whether they understand how to correctly use the vocabulary words in the correct context.

Differentiation

- **English language support—**Allow students to draw information that they have researched about camel caravans. Have students label their drawings.
- **Below-level students—**Review students' findings to check for comprehension and to guide them in identifying essential vocabulary.
- **Above-level students—**Have students sort the ten words into categories and share their ideas with the rest of the group.

Name________________________________

Facts About Camel Caravans

Read the passage. Then fill in the boxes below with information from the passage.

Camel caravans were an ancient form of transportation. It was a way for people to move goods from one place to another. Camel caravans were used mostly in the desert in North Africa. Camels traveled about 40 miles each day. They carried tea, spices, salt, and cloth.

There were many advantages and disadvantages to this type of travel. One main difficulty was the loss of camels. Some animals did not survive the trip. The heat and conditions were extreme in the desert. The trip also took a long time.

Yet there were also benefits to this type of travel. Camels could carry a lot of goods. They could also travel for a long time without water. Because of camel caravans, towns and centers were created along the most popular routes. These towns provided services. The camels and the people on the caravan could get food and supplies.

Benefits of Using Camels to Move Goods	Cargo that Camels Carried
Difficulties with Camel Caravan	**Effects on Life in North Africa**

Name________________________________

Essential Vocabulary

DIRECTIONS Read the passage *Facts About Camel Caravans.* Then use this sheet to record the ten important words. Some may be the focus vocabulary words you have already learned. Then write a summary of the passage.

Important Words:	

Summary:

___

___

___

___

___

___

___

Name________________________________

Camel Caravans Context Completion

DIRECTIONS Read each context completion sentence starter. Fill in the blank with information that correctly completes the sentence.

1. **Sentence starter:** One benefit of a camel *caravan* is ____

____

____

2. **Sentence starter:** *Transportation* during ancient times can be described as ____

____

____

3. **Sentence starter:** One *benefit* in the creation of new trade routes is that ____

____

____

4. **Sentence starter:** Examples of *cargo* that camels would carry include ____

____

____

Answer Key

The World According to Roald Dahl (Page 40)

1. Some stories Roald Dahl wrote include *Matilda*, *James and the Giant Peach*, and *Charlie and the Chocolate Factory*.
2. Students' responses will vary.

Related Words (Page 41)

Word	Word Part	Definition
autobiography	auto	self
	bio	life
	graph	writing
biography	bio	life
	graph	writing

The similarities between autobiography and biography are that they are both about the life of a person. The difference is that one is written by the person whom it is about.

Yes-No-Why?: Autobiography and Biography (Page 42)

Students' responses will vary. Suggested answers include:

1. This makes sense because a person's life is being told according to the order of time.
2. This seems illogical because an autobiography may have more than one character.
3. This does not make sense because a biography is not written by the person whom it is about.
4. This makes sense because readers may best examine a person's life by reading expository text, because it explains things in the person's life.

Informational Links (Page 46)

Students' responses will vary.

Personal Examples on Directions (Page 47)

Students' responses will vary. Suggested answers include:

1. I might need *directions* getting to a friend's house.
2. A time when I wrote a *list* was right before I went to the grocery store with my parents.
3. A time when something must happen in *sequential order* is when you are retelling a story. You must start from the beginning and go to the end.
4. A difference I noticed between *informational text* and *fictional text* is that informational text is nonfiction.

Elements of a Fantasy Story (Page 51)

Students' responses will vary.

Fantasy Context Interpretation (Page 52)

Students' responses will vary. Suggested answers include:

1. The reader might be nervous and scared for the main character.
2. The mother might be worried about how the toddler is going to behave.
3. The reader might be very anxious to see how the story ends.
4. The class might be very excited about writing fantasy.

Opening Day (Page 55)

1. This story is fiction.
2. Some examples are how Madison is acting. For example, she is nervous, anxious, and thrilled.

Answer Key *(cont.)*

Vocabulary Diagram: Fiction (Page 56)
Students' responses will vary.

Show You Know About Fiction (Page 57)
Students' responses will vary. Suggested answers include:

1. It was easy to *identify* the *mood* of the character based on how grouchy the author depicted her to be.
2. The *tone* of the story was easy to *identify* since the setting took place in a library.
3. The *fiction* story was not real whereas the *nonfiction* story was real.
4. The *tone* of the story and the setting were big indicators that the story was *fiction*.
5. Even though *nonfiction* books are true, readers will react to the *mood* they create.

The Lion and the Mouse (Page 60)

1. The conflicts were that the mouse was caught by the lion, and then the lion was caught by the hunters.
2. This passage is considered a fable because it has animals depicting human characteristics.

Reflections on Fables (Page 61)
Students' responses will vary.

Fable Word Translations (Page 62)
Students' responses will vary. Suggested answers include:

1. A *fable* is a *story* that is shared from generation to generation.
2. The lesson of a *fable* usually occurs at the end of the *story*.
3. *Fables* are important stories that can be shared with family members.
4. An important part of a *story* can be a disagreement.
5. The lesson of a *fable* is different than the main idea of a *story*.

A Personal Narrative (Page 65)
Students' responses will vary.

Vocabulary Diagram: Narrative (Page 66)
Students' responses will vary.

Personal Narrative Context Interpretation (Page 67)
Students' responses will vary. Suggested answers include:

1. The speaker might feel very proud to be a part of a personal narrative.
2. The friends might feel that having a conflict over a toy is ridiculous.
3. The students might be frustrated and not understanding the main idea.
4. The little girl might be excited to read the story.

How to Write with Descriptive Language (Page 70)
Students' responses will vary.

Answer Key *(cont.)*

Descriptive Writing Practice (Page 71)

Students' responses will vary, but students should integrate descriptive language into their writing.

Show You Know About Descriptive Writing (Page 72)

Students' responses will vary. Suggested answers include:

1. *Figurative language* is a tool authors use to help readers *visualize* characters.
2. When authors include *details* in their writing, it helps readers *visualize* a clear image.
3. Using a *figure of speech* is an alternative to *describing* something.
4. The *figurative language* used throughout the story conveyed a lot of *detail*.
5. Using a *figure of speech* allows authors to show *detail* in a different way.

Completing Sentences (Page 75)

1. body
2. signature
3. organize
4. Students' responses will vary.
5. Students' responses will vary.
6. Students' responses will vary.

Your Friendly Letter (Page 76)

Students' responses will vary but should include the parts of a letter.

Letter Word Translations (Page 77)

Students' responses will vary. Suggested answers include:

1. After I write my letter, I will write my name at the end.
2. The text of a letter comes after the salutation.
3. Why is the date included in a letter?
4. If I am writing to someone I know well, I can use a friendly conclusion.
5. Make sure to gather your ideas before writing a letter.

Writing Plan (Page 80)

Students' responses will vary.

Making Content Links (Page 81)

Students' responses will vary.

Personal Examples About Expository Texts (Page 82)

Students' responses will vary. Suggested answers include:

1. I might have to *explain* a mathematical problem at school.
2. A time I *clarified* something for someone was when they did not understand my instructions on how to build the model.
3. I used *expository* writing when I had to inform my classmates on my science project.
4. A type of text that is written to *inform* is a newspaper.
5. I once *instructed* my brother on how to make a peanut butter and jelly sandwich.

Similes Galore! (Page 85)

Students' responses will vary.

Answer Key *(cont.)*

Poetry Sample (Page 86)

Students' responses will vary.

Poetry Context Completion (Page 87)

Students' responses will vary. Suggested answers include:

1. Using a simile in poetry helps a reader to imagine by visualizing the picture.
2. A simile makes a comparison by using the words *like* and *as*.
3. To understand the truth and literal meaning of a poem that includes descriptive writing, you have to understand what is being described.
5. The use of descriptive language in poetry is very important for the reader because it helps imagine and visualize what the author is saying.

Multiplication Problems (Page 90)

Students' responses will vary.

Making Connections (Page 91)

Students' responses will vary.

Show You Know About Multiplication (Page 92)

Students' responses will vary. Suggested answers include:

1. To understand the *symbol* in multiplication will result in being able to solve the *operation*.
2. When you *multiply* two numbers, you must include an X as a multiplication *symbol* in your number sentence.
3. Division and multiplication have a similiar *relationships* of *operations*.
4. A multiplication *operation* requires you to *multiply* two numbers.
5. A mathematical *symbol* in a number sentence will *explain* what operation is used.

Dividing It All Up (Page 95)

1. The dividend is 15. The divisor is 3. $15 \div 3 = 5$.
2. The dividend is 24. The divisor is 6. $24 \div 6 = 4$.
3. The dividend is 18. The divisor is 2. $18 \div 2 = 9$.

Dividend, Divisor, and Quotient (Page 96)

Students' drawings will vary.

$21 \div 3 = 7$

$20 \div 2 = 10$

$12 \div 6 = 2$

Yes-No-Why?: Division (Page 97)

Students' responses will vary. Suggested answers include:

1. This does make sense because a division equation does include both.
2. This does not make sense because there are many other ways to solve a division word problem such as using manipulatives.
3. This seems logical because every time you solve a math problem you need some kind of strategy.
4. This does make sense because a quotient is a whole-number answer to a division problem.

Shape Attributes (Page 100)

Name of 3-D Shape	Number of Edges	Number of Faces	Real-World Example
cube	12	6	dice
cylinder	2	3	can
sphere	0	1	ball

Shapes in the Real World (Page 101)

Students' responses will vary.

Answer Key *(cont.)*

Personal Examples of 3-D Shapes (Page 102)

Students' responses will vary.

Drawing Fractions (Page 105)

Students' drawings will vary.

Vocabulary Diagram: Fraction (Page 106)

Students' responses will vary.

Fraction Word Translations (Page 107)

Students' responses will vary. Suggested answers include:

1. The numbers below the line of the two fractions were different even though the fractions themselves were the same in value.
2. A part of a number that is not a whole number is always written on top of the denominator.
3. Just because the numerators are the same, does not mean the fractions are equal.
4. A number that is not a whole number is written with both a number on top that represents the number of parts of the whole being considered, and as a number on bottom that is a number of parts making up the whole.

Picking Coins (Page 110)

Students' responses will vary.

Decimal Word Reflections (Page 111)

Students' responses will vary.

Decimal Context Completion (Page 112)

Students' responses will vary. Suggested answers include:

1. A cent and a dollar are related because they are both terms that describe money.
2. A decimal point is needed when solving a problem using money because it helps to keep the money amounts aligned when solving the problem.
3. One way to calculate the amount of money you have is add all your money.
4. Solving a word problem using cents requires a decimal point because cents are units of currency that are one hundredth of a dollar.

Experiences with the Water Cycle (Page 115)

Students' responses will vary.

Vocabulary Diagram: Water Cycle (Page 116)

Students' responses will vary.

Water Cycle Context Completion (Page 117)

Students' responses will vary. Suggested answers include:

1. The water cycle is continuous because it is a never ending cycle.
2. Condensation is the process of vapor losing heat and changing into a liquid.
3. One way to measure precipitation is to use a rain gauge.
4. The process of evaporation happens when something changes from a liquid to a vapor.

Answer Key *(cont.)*

Earth and the Moon (Page 120)

Students' Venn diagram will vary.

Earth *orbits* the sun and the *moon* orbits Earth. It takes about 27 days for the moon to orbit Earth and 365 days or a *year* for Earth to orbit the *sun*.

Parts of the Solar System (Page 121)

Students' responses will vary.

Solar System Context Interpretation (Page 122)

Students' responses will vary. Suggested answers include:

1. The scientists were probably thrilled to have discovered new planets.
2. The family feels very lucky to see something so interesting in the sky that will not appear for a long time.
3. The people were probably excited to have seen such a cool video.
4. The girl feels happy to have seen something so interesting.

Adaptations in Nature (Page 125)

Students' responses will vary.

Connecting to What You Know (Page 126)

Students' responses will vary.

Yes-No-Why?: Survival (Page 127)

Students' responses will vary. Suggested answers include:

1. This makes sense because adaptations help animals survive.
2. This makes sense because an environment is a type of place where plants and animals live.
3. This seems illogical because animals in all kinds of climates can detect their prey.
4. This seems logical because humans can certainly destroy habitats and cause animals to face endangerment or extinction.

Different States of Matter (Page 130)

Students' responses will vary.

Searching for Clues (Page 131)

Students' responses will vary.

Show You Know About States of Matter (Page 132)

Students' responses will vary. Suggested answers include:

1. *Gases* and *solids* are two different states of matter.
2. Objects that are examples of different *states of matter* may share similar *properties*.
3. A *liquid* is an example of a *state of matter* because it is one type of form that matter takes on.
4. One *property* of many objects that are *solid* is that they retain a certain shape.
5. *Gas* and *liquid* are different because a *liquid* is fluid and a *gas* goes everywhere.

Answer Key *(cont.)*

Investigation Work (Page 135)
Students' responses will vary.

Analyzing the Investigation (Page 136)
Students' responses will vary.

Personal Examples About Scientific Investigations (Page 137)
Students' responses will vary.

Labeling a Map (Page 140)

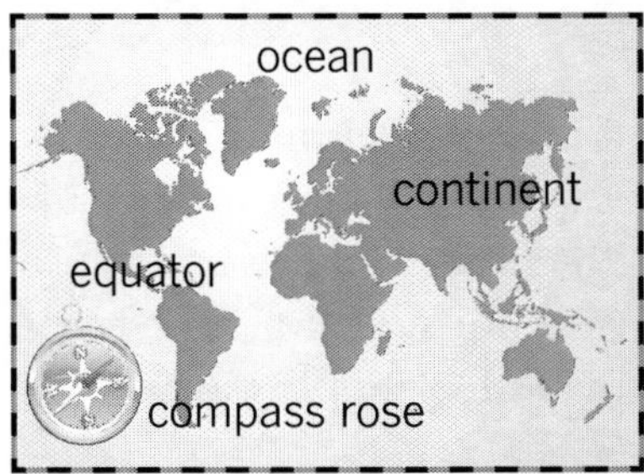

Personal Connections (Page 141)
Students' responses will vary.

Show You Know About a Map (Page 142)
Students' responses will vary. Suggested answers include:

1. A *world map* and a *globe* both show the whole planet.
2. A *key* on a *map* tells you what the symbols on the map represent.
3. Using a *globe* makes it easy to locate the seven *continents*.
4. The *key* and *compass rose* can help you read a map correctly.
5. The arrows on a *compass rose represent* the directions for north, south, east, and west.

Pick a Feature (Page 145)
Students' responses will vary.

Linking Ideas (Page 146)
Students' responses will vary.

Yes-No-Why?: Geographic Features (Page 147)
Students' responses will vary. Suggested answers include:

1. This makes sense because a desert is unique because it is so hot with very little rainfall, and not all plants can grow in those conditions.
2. This seems illogical because the plains are known for wide open spaces of flat land with very few trees.
4. This does not make sense because although an island is surrounded by water, a peninsula only has water on three sides.
5. This seems logical because trees are plentiful in the forest or mountain regions.

Equal Rights Web (Page 150)
Students' responses will vary.

Vocabulary Diagram: Equality (Page 151)
Students' responses will vary.

Personal Examples About Equality (Page 152)
Students' responses will vary.

Going on a Word Hunt (Page 156)
Students' responses will vary.

Answer Key *(cont.)*

Innovation Context Interpretation (Page 157)

Students' responses will vary. Suggested answers include:

1. She was impressed by the industry's productivity.
2. People are curious about what kind of shoe was made and how it looks.
3. People are very interested in this invention because cars cause a great deal of pollution.
4. The teacher is thrilled that his students are learning so much and doing so well.

Facts About Camel Caravans (Page 160)

Students' responses will vary. Suggested answers include:

1. Benefits of using camels to move goods: able to move more goods, camels used to desert climate and conditions
2. Cargo that camels carried: wool, cotton fabrics, tea, silk, beads, ceramics, utensils
3. Difficulties with camel caravan: still slow moving, required handlers to walk with camels, camels often collapsed from fatigue
4. Effects on life in North Africa: more movement of goods, small towns along the route developed since caravans needed to stop during the journey

Essential Vocabulary (Page 161)

Students' responses will vary.

Context Completion (Page 162)

Students' responses will vary. Suggested answers include:

1. One benefit of a camel caravan is that the camel could carry more cargo than a human traveler.
2. Transportation during ancient times can be described as practical and innovative.
3. One benefit in the creation of new trade routes is that Northern Africa had a positive effect on that region because new cities were formed along the trade route to provide for people passing through.
4. Examples of cargo that camels would carry include tea, silk, and wool.

References Cited

Beck, I.L., M.G. McKeown, and L. Kucan. 2002. *Bringing words to life: Robust vocabulary instruction.* New York: Guilford Press.

Cunningham, A.E., and K.E. Stanovich. 1998. What reading does for the mind. *American Educator*, 22 (1–2), 8–15.

Feldman, K., and K. Kinsella. 2005. *Narrowing the language gap: The case for explicit vocabulary instruction.* New York: Scholastic.

Graves, M.F. 2000. A vocabulary program to complement and bolster a middle grade comprehension program. In B. M. Taylor, M. F. Graves, and P. van den Broek, Eds. *Reading for meaning: Fostering comprehension in the middle grades* (116–135). Newark, DE: International Reading Association.

Lehr, F., J. Osborn, and E.H. Hiebert. 2004. *A focus on vocabulary.* Honolulu, HI: Pacific Resources for Education and Learning.

Marzano, R.J. 2004. *Building background knowledge for academic achievement.* Alexandria, VA: Association for Supervision and Curriculum Development.

Nagy, W. 2005. Why vocabulary instruction needs to be long-term and comprehensive. In *Teaching and learning vocbulary: Bringing research to practice*, ed. E. H. Hiebert and M. L. Kamil, 27–44. Mahwah, N.J.: Erlbaum.

Nagy, W.E., and J.A. Scott. 2000. Vocabulary processes. In Volume 3 of *Handbook of reading research*, ed. E. H. Hiebert and M. L. Kamil, 27–44. Mahwah, N.J.: Erlbaum.

Yopp, H., K. Yopp, and A. Bishop. 2009. *Vocabulary instruction for academic success.* Huntington Beach, CA: Shell Education.

Sample Word Lists

These sample word lists are meant to serve as examples. They are intended to help teachers create their own lists of general academic words and specialized content words for each grade level or within each unit of study.

General Academic Words

advantage
allow
always
appear
apply
basic
beginning
belief
category
cause
center
change
characteristic
clarify
compare
component
concept
content
contrast
copy
create
define
describe
detail
develop
directions
disadvantage
draw
effect
element
emphasize
ending
enhance
examine
explain
fact
familiar
form
identify
illustrate
improve
include
influence
instructions
interpret
label
likely
list
main
meaning
notice
observation
order
persuade
precede
predict
produce
purpose
recognize
record
relationship
represent

Sample Word Lists *(cont.)*

result

review

show

significant

solve

source

specific

strategy

study

successful

support

throughout

topic

type

various

Specialized Content Words

Language Arts

author

autobiography

biography

character

composition

consonant

descriptive writing

drama

expository

expository text

fable

fantasy

fiction

figurative language

figure of speech

foreshadow

grammar

greeting

letter

mood

moral

narrative

nonfiction

perspective

phrase

plot

poem

poetry

prewriting

signature

simile

story

syllable

tone

Mathematics

calculate

cent

coordinate system

cube

cylinder

decimal

denominator

divide

dividend

divisor

dollar

equivalent

fraction

inverse

measurement

multiple

number line

Sample Word Lists *(cont.)*

numerator
operation
pattern
quotient
shape
simplify
sphere
symbol
three-dimensional
two-dimensional

Science

adaption
animals
condensation
evaporation
food chain
fossils
gas
habitat
hypothesis
investigation
liquid
magnet
mineral
moon
orbit
organism
planet
plants
precipitation
reproduction
solar system
states of matter

Social Studies

ancient
boycott
caravan
cargo
civil rights
compass rose
community
continent
desert
Earth
environment
equal rights
forest
globe
heritage
hero
immigrant
industry
invention
manufacture
oceans
peninsula
plains
protest
region
rotation
solid
territory
trade
tradition
transportation

Contents of the Teacher Resource CD

Student Activity Pages

Page	Title	Filename
	Reading	
40	The World According to Roald Dahl	page40.pdf
41	Related Words	page41.pdf
42	Yes-No-Why?: Autobiography and Biography	page42.pdf
45	How to Make a Berry Good Smoothie	page45.pdf
46	Informational Links	page46.pdf
47	Personal Examples on Directions	page47.pdf
50	The Rock	page50.pdf
51	Elements of a Fantasy Story	page51.pdf
52	Fantasy Context Interpretation	page52.pdf
55	Opening Day	page55.pdf
56	Vocabulary Diagram: Fiction	page56.pdf
57	Show You Know About Fiction	page57.pdf
60	The Lion and the Mouse	page60.pdf
61	Reflections on Fables	page61.pdf
62	Fable Word Translations	page62.pdf
	Writing	
65	A Personal Narrative	page65.pdf
66	Vocabulary Diagram: Narrative	page66.pdf
67	Personal Narrative Context Interpretation	page67.pdf
70	How to Write with Descriptive Language	page70.pdf
71	Descriptive Writing Practice	page71.pdf
72	Show You Know About Descriptive Writing	page72.pdf
75	Completing Sentences	page75.pdf
76	Your Friendly Letter	page76.pdf
77	Letter Word Translations	page77.pdf
80	Writing Plan	page80.pdf
81	Making Content Links	page81.pdf
82	Personal Examples About Expository Texts	page82.pdf
85	Similes Galore!	page85.pdf
86	Poetry Sample	page86.pdf
87	Poetry Context Completion	page87.pdf

Page	Title	Filename
	Mathematics	
90	Multiplication Problems	page90.pdf
91	Making Connections	page91.pdf
92	Show You Know About Multiplication	page92.pdf
95	Dividing It All Up	page95.pdf
96	Dividend, Divisor, and Quotient	page96.pdf
97	Yes-No-Why?: Division	page97.pdf
100	Shape Attributes	page100.pdf
101	Shapes in the Real World	page101.pdf
102	Personal Examples of 3-D Shapes	page102.pdf
105	Drawing Fractions	page105.pdf
106	Vocabulary Diagram: Fraction	page106.pdf
107	Fraction Word Translations	page107.pdf
110	Picking Coins	page110.pdf
111	Decimal Word Reflections	page111.pdf
112	Decimal Context Completion	page112.pdf

Contents of the Teacher Resource CD *(cont.)*

Student Activity Pages

Page	Title	Filename
Science		
115	Experiences with the Water Cycle	page115.pdf
116	Vocabulary Diagram: Water Cycle	page116.pdf
117	Water Cycle Context Completion	page117.pdf
120	Earth and the Moon	page120.pdf
121	Parts of the Solar System	page121.pdf
122	Solar System Context Interpretation	page122.pdf
125	Adaptations in Nature	page125.pdf
126	Connecting to What You Know	page126.pdf
127	Yes-No-Why?: Survival	page127.pdf
130	Different States of Matter	page130.pdf
131	Searching for Clues	page131.pdf
132	Show You Know About States of Matter	page132.pdf
135	Investigation Work	page135.pdf
136	Analyzing the Investigation	page136.pdf
137	Personal Examples About Scientific Investigations	page137.pdf

Page	Title	Filename
Social Studies		
140	Labeling a Map	page140.pdf
141	Personal Connections	page141.pdf
142	Show You Know About a Map	page142.pdf
145	Pick a Feature	page145.pdf
146	Linking Ideas	page146.pdf
147	Yes-No-Why?: Geographic Features	page147.pdf
150	Equal Rights Web	page150.pdf
151	Vocabulary Diagram: Equality	page151.pdf
152	Personal Examples About Equality	page152.pdf
155	Industrial Revolution	page155.pdf
156	Going on a Word Hunt	page156.pdf
157	Innovation Context Interpretation	page157.pdf
160	Facts About Camel Caravans	page160.pdf
161	Essential Vocabulary	page161.pdf
162	Camel Caravans Context Completion	page162.pdf